RAWGE JONES

DON'T TELL MOM

a Farm Boy Memoir

Contents

Preface v

Acknowledgments viii

1 The Big Heist 1

2 YOLO 17

3 A Pigeon Named Homer 21

4 Keep It Short, Rawge 31

5 Grace and Well-Chosen Words 35

6 Writers & Readers 39

7 Zen Morning 43

8 Foul-Mouths and Footballs 53

9 Who is the Smartest Person in the World? 61

10 Born to Snarl 65

11 Not a Lick of Common Sense 75

12 Butterflies & Busted Stitches 87

13 Life is Too Short for Whining 95

14 Bull Riders & Momma's Boys 99

15 Idiots 107

16 It's Clearing Up 111

17 Bad Haiku 117

18 Music is Magic 119

19 Support the Arts 125

20 From Grit to Shine 133

21 Magnification 137

22 Burdens & Baggage 141

23 A Simple Choice 145

24 Just Do Something 151

25 My Rescue Story   155
26 The Forty-Year Lesson   163
27 That Still Small Voice   171
28 The Hunderds   175
29 A Teaching Moment   183
30 What Can I Do?   187
31 A Fishing Story   191
32 Nashville Style   197
33 Reboot My Heart   201
34 The Mexican   205
35 Odds Are   211
36 Dreams   219
37 Fight or Flight   223
38 You're Dead to Me   229
39 Ready to Fight   231
40 Memory Seeds   233
41 Angels Among Us   235
42 Home   239
About the Author   242
Also by Rawge Jones   243

Preface

I want to live forever.

I will. In Heaven.

But I'm greedy. I want to live forever, here.

Well, I can't. I won't. I know that. I will live only as long as I live. No less. No more. I'm not in charge. But I'm smart. Smart enough to know that my death will likely be sooner, rather than later. Heck, I've got my own personal vulture that lurks and follows me around. There hasn't been a day in the past five years that it hasn't glided by overhead and looked me over. It's kind of creepy, but I accept it.

I've had and still have problems. Death has already knocked at my door and touched me with its icy fingers. Yes, I've been there. Doctors have explained some of the realities. I'm sure I've been spared many of them. But I can read. I have the internet. I know the reality and depth of my disease.

Still, I want to live forever.

In a hundred years, I want my name to come up in someone's conversation. I want a child to say Rawge or Papa or even just to think about the old man with the long hair and cowboy hat.

But I know I'll someday die, and my memories could die with me. All of them, even the most amazing moments in my life.

Waking up in a strange bed, in a strange country and place, rubbing my eyes and having to remember where I am.

I love those memories, but they could be gone.

Opening my eyes with sweaty hair hanging in my face. Squinting to see Rhonda, my love, standing at a sun-drenched window of a new land.

Those could pass away.

My mind remembering me standing beside her, holding her, to watch the sun ease its way up from an ocean's horizon.

Those are precious and vivid memories. They are mine. They are in my heart. But those could be gone as well.

Others, too. Brothers and sisters, loving one another. Schoolyard fights and first girlfriends. The first time I saw an ocean and the first time I rode a horse. A puppy that grew into a dog that never left my side.

Many others.

But still, I want to live forever.

So, I've fought it. I've written books. I've filled them with memories. They're full of my successes and failures, my best times and worst. The books and their pages can outlive me.

I've told stories to family and friends. I've crafted them rich with detail and color. They can be retold a thousand times, for a thousand years.

If I am blessed, a grandchild or a great-grandchild will find a dusty copy of one of my books in an attic and ask, "Who is this?" In my heart, I want someone to remember me enough to look at the photo on the cover and say, "That is your great-great grandpapa." I want them to open the book and say, "Look at this chapter, that's about your great-great grandmommy. Wasn't she beautiful?" There, in that moment, I can live. I'll be the life in the words on a page and a young person's sepia memory of an adventurous cowboy and the love of his life.

You want that, too. I know, because everyone does.

We all want to live forever.

So, my friends...

Take photos. Write a book. Tell stories of a life well lived. Don't hide the mistakes. Recognize and revel in the blessings. Never, ever, stop making memories with everyone around you and pull them into your story.

And just in case everything else fails...

Plant a tree with someone.

Yes, plant a tree that can live three lifetimes. Plant an oak. Plant something that a hundred years from now, a child can play in a swing beneath its branches and tell their friends, "My great papa planted this tree." Plant a tree that, a century from now, lovers can sit under its shade and look into each other's dreamy eyes and make their own memories. Plant a tree that someday, when we're dead and gone, it will still drop its seeds and make new trees.

Yes, plant a tree.

I'm gonna live forever in Heaven.

But I can live forever here, in words and stories, pictures and memories.

And, in the humbleness of the rings in a tree.

Acknowledgments

I can't fully express my gratitude to Rhonda for her hard work and vast knowledge. Her "know-how" in many areas, from editing to cover design to publishing, has been invaluable. I'm endlessly thankful for her unwavering dedication and support. Even more so, she's my muse and partner in everything life brings.

I'm also deeply humbled and honored that my friends Karen, Chris and Mary have again given up their time to offer valuable editing insights (okay, corrections!), thoughtful perspectives, and continued encouragement.

I am incredibly fortunate! Thank you all so much!

1

The Big Heist

Most everyone has a time in their lives when they feel like they need to make a change and be better. Maybe there's guilt gnawing at them, or there's shame hanging over their heads. Maybe we've managed to see into the future and didn't like what we saw. Statistics tell us that most of these critical life moments happen when we are in our thirties. Sometimes forty or even fifty. But sometimes it's when we're ten.

"Where you going, Dad?"

"I'm going to a ranch over in Kings County. A guy's got a bunch of cotton tarps for sale. I'll be over there for a few hours."

"I want to go."

"No, I'll probably stay there and listen to the ball game with some of the guys for a while, but there's nothing for you to do over there."

"There's nothing for me to do here."

"Well, there's less over there."

"Just park us in the shade, and I'll sit in the truck and read my book. I just want to go somewhere. I'm tired of sitting around here."

Pops looked off in the distance for a minute. "Okay. Get a book. But don't cause me any trouble."

"I won't. I promise."

We lived in Fresno County, but right near the line with Kings County. Other than to go to the stores in Hanford or to visit Grandma and Papa in Lemoore, I didn't know much about the rest of the county. So, I just sat back and watched out the open window as we drove. I don't know what I expected, but there wasn't much to see that was any different from where we lived. There were cotton fields on both sides of the road, and every mile or so, there was a house set back off the road. Every house had a cow or two or a horse or two in a shoddy pen. Some of them had big shade trees but many of them didn't have as much as a bush or a blade of grass. Both trees and grass took water, and sometimes water was hard to come by in the dusty valley. Water was saved for the thirsty cotton fields. Some folks couldn't waste it on trees or grass unless a cow could eat it.

We started the trip on paved roads with names, but before long, we had turned onto dusty dirt roads. Pops was absorbed in a ball game on the radio. We had driven about forty-five minutes, and other than Dad's occasional cussing at a bad play, he had hardly spoken a word. I was getting bored and was starting to regret my pleading to tag along. I had envisioned a fun drive through new country with Pops telling me who lived where and pointing out every landmark. I figured we'd at least drive through a new town or two, stop somewhere for a Coke, and maybe I'd get a hamburger. At this point in the drive, we may have well been the last car in a funeral procession, except there was no crying, just a baseball game playing.

Ten minutes of sitting is a long time for a kid. Thirty minutes is forever, and an hour is an eternity. Just as I contemplated opening the door and jumping out, I saw a big ranch coming into view. Finally! As we pulled through a long driveway bordered by tamarack trees, I scanned the trees and buildings. There were the typical shop buildings that you see on every ranch, but there were other buildings, too. There were big two-story barracks like we once had at our place. They were there to house the hundreds of men who arrived at cotton-picking season before the mechanical cotton pickers put them all out of work. There were a bunch of long buildings with windows and one office building that looked faintly like the front of an old train station.

As promised, Dad slid the truck in between a couple of trees, in the shade. He ran his fingers through his hair, slicked it back a bit, and wiped his face with his hand.

"I'll be in there. That's their office." He pointed to a square building about the size of a small house with a swamp-cooler's low hum coming from the square metal box that hung on most every building in the valley. That was the only thing that made being indoors bearable.

I pointed to the building with a big porch and official-looking doors. "What's that other building? That's not the office?"

"It used to be. I don't know what it is now. Just sit in here and read your book. Don't go wandering around. You can play the radio a little, just don't run the battery down. I'll be an hour or so."

He turned and gave me the look. We made eye contact, and I nodded. He meant business. Stay in the truck, and don't go wandering around.

I watched him disappear through the front door without knocking. For the few seconds that the door was open, I could hear men laughing and the baseball game blaring from a radio. I crawled halfway out of the open window and sat with my feet in the truck and my head above the top of the cab to get a good look around. It was pretty much as I'd seen driving in, except there were a couple of houses about a quarter mile away. I heard no voices, no trucks or tractors, not even a barking dog. The place seemed deserted, except for the five or six trucks parked around the office.

I took my book from my green knapsack and looked at the cover. *Where The Red Fern Grows - A Story of Two Dogs and a Boy*, by Wilson Rawls. I had just checked it out at our little town's library. The librarian, whose opinion I respected tremendously, had handed it to me the moment I walked through the library door just a few days before. She stuck the book in my direction and said, "Rawge, you've got to read this. You will love it!" The look on her face was all it took. I walked out with it tucked under my arm.

I slumped down in the seat, resting against the door, and studied the book's cover for a minute—a painting of a boy next to a big tree trunk with a couple of happy dogs playing at his feet. I turned to page one. But before I read a single word, I heard the first real sound I'd heard since Pops closed the office door behind him. It was a faint, clickety sound, but it disappeared quickly. I raised back up from my seat to look around. I looked toward each building and even the houses in the distance but saw nothing moving. I looked the whole place over again, but still nothing.

I'd no sooner gotten comfortable in the seat when I heard it again. This time, I got up quicker and saw a flash of a kid on a bicycle disappear behind one of the long buildings a hundred yards away. I leaned out of the window, waiting for him to come around the other side. A minute or two went by, but the bike didn't reappear. Dad's warning to stay in the truck and not wander around was still fresh in my mind, but I opened the truck door anyway. I stepped out and glanced toward the office. The door was still closed. The only window had a shade, so I felt bold about getting out of the truck.

I crouched down low like a soldier in a combat movie and scurried over to the building, following the path of the bicycle. As I rounded the corner to the back of the building, I startled a kid about my own age as he wedged a screwdriver into the building's old casement window.

"Shit! You scared me!"

"Sorry. I was just coming to see who you are."

"Well, who are you?"

"I'm Rawge. My dad's here to buy something. Who are you?"

"Sammy."

"You live here?"

"Yeah. Over there." He motioned with his head toward the houses.

"Where do you live?"

I glanced around, not even sure where I lived. I pointed towards the west. "That way, I think. What are you doing?"

"I'm opening this window so I can get in and play pool. I do it all the time when I get bored."

"They got a pool table in there?"

"Yeah, and lots of other stuff."

I watched as he pried on the window until it was opened enough that he could grasp the end of it with his hands. Once he had it in his grip, he shook it violently back and forth. I watched as the crank on the inside slowly turned at the force of the shaking window. Once it was open a few inches, he bent his arm and stuck it through the narrow opening. Slowly, he turned the crank with his fingertips, and in under a minute, the window was open. He motioned with his head, and we both climbed in.

It was dark inside, but I could see a pool table, a ping-pong table, a bench, and barbells. Over in a corner, chairs were sitting around a small table, with a deck of cards scattered in the middle.

"What is this place?"

"I guess there used to be a lot of grown men that lived here. But now, no one hardly comes in here. I used to come in here with my cousin, but he moved. You wanna play pool?"

"I can't. My dad told me to stay in the truck and wait for him. If he catches me out of the truck, he'll probably whip my ass."

"Is he over there?" He pointed toward the office building.

"Yeah. I think they're listening to the ball game."

"Yeah, my dad's there too. He took a six-pack. I wonder what inning it is?"

"I don't know, but I'd better get back to the truck."

I stepped toward the window, but Sammy stopped me. "The window is for getting in. We can leave out the front door."

He closed up the casement window without locking it, then cracked open the front door. He gave a quick peek around, and we walked out. Sammy followed me as I headed straight back to Dad's truck. Once we were there and I was safe, I quietly put the tailgate down, and we took a seat.

We sat on the tailgate with feet swinging and asked each other questions. Sammy was in the same grade, but he went to a school that I'd never heard of. Just like me, he'd lived on the same ranch since he was born. He said he didn't like books much, but his favorite TV show was *Gilligan's Island*. He told me that he was born here but that his dad came from Michoacan, somewhere in Mexico. He said it was by the ocean. He'd seen pictures. He spoke good Spanish, and we laughed every time I tried to say something in Spanish. He quizzed me by pointing to things.

He pointed a finger at a tree.

"Arbol."

He pointed to his shoe.

"Zapato."

He pointed to his leg.

"Piedra."

"No, that's a rock! It's pierna!"

We both laughed.

Sammy abruptly interrupted our laughter. "Hey, you want to see something else? It's over there." He motioned to the official-looking building with the train station facade.

"What is it?"

"I can't tell you. I can only show you. Come on, we'll hurry."

I was intrigued enough to look over toward the office door. There was still no sign of movement, just the constant drone of the swamp cooler.

"Okay, let's go, but we've got to hurry."

We hopped off the tailgate and walked toward the building, but halfway there, Sammy ducked back under some trees, walked behind the building, and waited by the far side. He looked around carefully, then motioned for us to go. We ran around the side, opened the front door, and stepped in. Sammy closed the door, and I looked around. There were nice benches along both walls and a Coke machine in the corner. At the front, there was a big teller's window with a counter like you see in a bank. I had seen it before. I knew that years before, this was where the big groups of men showed up each day, gave their names at the window, and got paid in dollar bills.

I looked around at the window and the high ceiling. "Yep, pretty cool."

"No! This isn't it. It's behind that door."

Before I could say another word, Sammy had the little screwdriver out of his pocket and was shimmying the lock on the door. A few seconds and it popped open. This wasn't un-ordinary, I could open every door and lock on our ranch with anything from a screwdriver to a bobby pin, but I admired his speed.

We stepped in, and Sammy swept both his arms and open hands towards the side wall with a bit of a magician's "ta-da!" I looked in the direction of his sweeping hands, and there it was, a huge black safe door with a big dial and beautiful fancy gold writing scrolled on the front—American Safety. The safe was built into the wall, but the big door was about four feet wide and tall enough for a man to walk through. It was beautiful and something like I'd seen on TV but never in real life.

"What's inside?"

"I don't know. Probly a million dollars."

"Well, step back, and I'll have that thing open in no time."

"Shut up!"

"Seriously! I can crack a safe. Step back and let me work my magic."

Sammy stood back, crossed his arms, and said, "It's all yours."

A couple of weeks before, I had watched a crime show on TV. One of the criminals wanted to crack a safe and told his fellow criminals that safes were very difficult to open, even if you know their elaborate combinations. He explained that there were three hundred and sixty tiny dots on the dial and that in the process of going from one direction to the other, if you missed by one dot, it wouldn't open. Then you'd have to start over. Three full turns to the right. Stop on the first number. Then, back one full turn to the left, passing the first number. Stop on the second number. Then turn the dial in the other direction and stop on the precise number. If you missed anything by a fraction of a dot, it wouldn't open. So, the criminal thief told his criminal friends that no one does that anymore because when the door gets closed, all they do is turn the handle two dots to the left to lock it back. Now, all you had to do to open it was turn the dial back two dots to the right.

I stepped up to the big black door and made a spectacle of putting my hands together and cracking my knuckles. I shielded Sammy's vision of the safe door with my body, cocked my ear like I was listening for tumblers to click, and made fake motions of turning the dial. After a minute, I turned the dial two clicks to the right.

"Voila!" I turned the handle, and the safe door opened.

I turned to look at Sammy. He was wide-eyed with an ear-to-ear grin.

"Damn! You cracked it!"

"Of course I did. Are you ready to look inside?"

We both walked up to the door. I grabbed the handle and slowly pulled the heavy door open. Once the light broke inside, we got a faint first look at the hidden treasures. The vault was big enough that we could walk inside, so we stepped in. There was a light switch just inside the door, so I clicked it. A small bulb in the top of the vault came on, revealing the safe's contents. With great anticipation, we both slowly looked from side to side and floor to ceiling. But there were no gold bars or stacks of Krugerrands. There were no treasure boxes of diamonds or gems shining in the light. There were no piles of old precious documents or maps or anything else that would pop into the heads of a couple of ten-year-old safe crackers. It was a glorified closet!

The vault had several cases of soda stacked on the floor, waiting for their time to get loaded into the Coke machine in the front lobby. There were boxes of light bulbs and a mop bucket. Piled at the back were some boxes of typewriter paper, and a couple of small boxes sat on a shelf just beside the door. Sammy and I looked at each other with disgust.

"It's a damn closet!"

"Damn. It is. Let's go."

Just before I flicked the light off, I opened the corner of one of the small, narrow boxes by the door. Well, there it was—the treasure. There were about fifty sets of rolled-up coins, undoubtedly the profit of the lone Coke machine in the other room. I looked at Sammy, then grabbed a roll of quarters and stuck it in my pocket. I don't know where the reflex came from. I had never stolen anything in my life. Maybe it was the dark side of my mind telling me, "You just cracked a safe, and you ain't leaving here with nothin' to show for it." Whatever it was, I grabbed the quarters. Sammy looked at me and did the same. I clicked off the light, closed the door, and turned the dial two dots to the left. We hustled through the other door, locked it, and gingerly stepped back out into the sunlight. In a few quick steps, we were again safely sitting on the tailgate of Pop's truck.

We sat in silence for a minute. There was adrenaline involved. We had near-accidentally pulled off a heist. My heart was pounding.

Sammy looked me in the eyes. "Don't ever tell nobody."

"I won't. You either."

"I won't."

The fun was over. In an instant, we had become criminals. It changed everything. Sammy walked toward his bike, took one last look back, nodded, and rode off. I hopped off the tailgate and walked to the truck door. I crawled in and stuck the roll of quarters way down in the bottom of my knapsack. I pulled my book out just in time to hear the office door open, and Dad stepped out. He said goodbye to the other men and got in the truck. He was in a jovial mood.

"The Giants won. Did you finish your book?"

"No, I've still got some reading to do."

"What's it about?"

With no baseball game to listen to and likely a couple of beers under his belt, he wanted to talk. But I was in no mood. I just wanted to sit there and keep my mouth shut before I blurted out that I was a thief.

"It's about a boy raising a couple of dogs."

He asked a couple more questions that I faintly answered. He asked if I was all right, and I told him that I wasn't feeling great. With that, he let me just sit. In an hour, we were home. I was relieved to get into my bedroom and stick the contraband quarters down in the bottom drawer of my clothes chest. It had winter clothes in it, so Mom wouldn't open it for months.

A few days passed, and the stolen quarters hardly left my mind. One side of my mind constantly berated the other side, even when I was asleep."Why would you do such a thing? What were you thinking? You're going to Hell."

I was no bible scholar, but I knew enough to know that stealing was a sin. In fact, I think God was pretty clear on the matter.

#8 - THOU SHALT NOT STEAL!

It was one of the big ones. It was chiseled in stone!

A few more days passed and I managed to think about it less. Maybe it would just fade away. But I guess it doesn't work that way. One afternoon, while I was lying on my bed, reading the story about a boy and his two dogs, my mom walked into the room carrying a load of clothes.

"I finally washed your two sweaters that have been in the bottom of the laundry basket. You sure look nice in that red one."

As luck would have it, Mom opened the bottom drawer and tucked in the two perfectly folded sweaters. She raised back up.

"You look good in the blue one too. Where'd you get a roll of quarters?"

Well, I was a safecracker and a thief. I was a hardened criminal and capable of most any deceit. But one thing I couldn't do was lie to my mom. This was it—my moment to get the whole ordeal off my chest. It might mean jail or even prison, but I was coming clean!

"I stole it."

Mom laughed for a minute. "Well, you're probably gonna go to Hell then." With a grin, she walked out of the room.

I could feel my face squirm into a puzzled look. At first, I was relieved. I didn't lie to my mom. I confessed to a pretty horrendous crime, and there were no repercussions. But then I was puzzled. Dang! My dear momma thinks that her sweet son is such a good kid that she can't even believe me when I confess! But then her reaction sunk in a little more. Maybe she *did* believe me, and maybe I *was* going to Hell!

I have to admit that as a kid, I'd spent an unreasonable amount of time thinking about Hell. Well, it was less about Hell and more about eternity. But the two seemed intermingled enough that I didn't want any part of it. And here I was with my dear, sweet momma telling me that's exactly where I was headed!

I left the roll of quarters in the drawer for the next week while I searched for a way to redeem my soul. The guilt was eating me up. It was like a nagging foxtail in my sock. It gnawed at me every minute of the day and night. There was a shame in the front of my mind that clouded everything. I couldn't even read a book without it creeping into my mind. I'd read two lines, and during the third line, my mind would say, "You're a thief!"

I couldn't concentrate at school without it jumping into my head. My teacher would write a line on the blackboard, and I'd read it as, "You're a thief, and you're gonna break your momma's heart!" Even when I watched TV, it wouldn't let me relax. I'd watch TV, and every *Gunsmoke* episode was Marshal Matt Dillon trying to catch some dirty, rotten thief!

I had to fix it. I reasoned that surely I wasn't the first criminal in the world who was ready to walk away from his life of crime and go straight. The ideal plan would have been to simply return the loot. But I knew that was nearly impossible. I didn't even know where the ranch building was, and even if I could get there, I'd run the risk of getting caught. I imagined having to explain that I was actually not stealing something but that I was merely returning something that I'd borrowed. Adding a lie to the equation didn't seem like a good start to my first steps on the straight and narrow path.

One night while lying in bed, I hit on a plan. If I couldn't return the dirty money, then I needed to use it for something good. Something really good. It needed to be something further in the good direction than the stealing was in the bad direction. Now, I just needed to think of something good!

My first thought was to give it to the little church in town. Maybe they could buy some paint and spruce the place up. I thought that maybe they could host a picnic, and a whole bunch of people could eat fried chicken and drink Cokes. But those thoughts didn't last long. The thought of a roll of stolen quarters landing in the tin offering plate actually made me a little sick to my stomach. Surely, the stained-glass window would shatter at the sound. Nope. I'd need a better idea.

Soon, I reasoned that if I couldn't give it directly to God, I would go in the other direction and give it to the poor. As I thought more about it, it seemed even better to give it to the poorest of the poor—the hobos that camped out on the edge of town behind the melon packing sheds. These men were so poor that they didn't even have a house! A roll of quarters might be just the thing one of them needed to put him on a new path in life. Just the thought of it all made me feel better. Suddenly I felt more like Robin Hood than that crooked John Dillinger. I finally felt a tinge of peace. As I fell asleep and said my goodnight prayers, I filled God in on my plan.

With my newly found sense of relief, I worked out the final details of the plan. The next time Mom was going into town to shop or visit her friends, I'd make it all happen. In less than a week, I was skipping down Main Street, heading for the packing sheds. I crossed the street at the railroad tracks, walked past McElroy's Farm Equipment Repair Shop, joined back up with the railroad tracks, and headed for the edge of town. Hobos could walk around town, but they were required to live on the fringes so that the good folks in town didn't have to look at them. Even back then, I understood the shaky truce between the "have very littles" and the "have nothings."

When I arrived at the last metal building at the packing plant, I expected to see a half dozen men sitting on crates, passing around a bottle of wine tightly wrapped in a paper sack. I'd just study them until one of them seemed to stand out as the most needy. Then I'd just walk up, stick out my handful of quarters, and announce that he's one step closer to leaving the hobo camp behind!

It was a good plan, except the place was devoid of hobos. They were usually propped up in the shade of a couple of big tanks. I had seen them many times. But on this day, the place was empty. I walked around a bit, just in case they'd moved. I circled each big tank, then walked back up both sides of the packing sheds. I saw some men working on machinery, but they weren't hobos. I could give the money to anyone, and I was sure they'd take it, but the redemptive value required me to put it squarely in the palm of someone with the greatest need. Robin Hood didn't grease the palm of Nottingham's elite. His filched bag of silver went to the poor.

I knew that I was not going to return home with the loot. Today I was going to unburden myself from my deed and be done with it. So, I needed to add some latitude to my plan. I decided that I would find a spot and loosely hide the money. When the first deserving hobo returned to the hobo spot, he would discover the quarters, turn his gaze to the heavens, and say, "Hallelujah! My prayers have been answered!"

Now I just needed to find the perfect hiding spot. It couldn't be so secluded that no one would find it but hidden enough that a kid loitering around wouldn't stumble on it. A kid would use it to buy stupid kid stuff. That wouldn't get me off the Hell hook. I walked around each tank again, then up the gravel road toward town. As I walked around, I saw a hint of a trail that seemed to be a shortcut around the packing sheds and toward the town's water tower. I had never noticed it before. I reasoned that this might be the path that hobos use to get into town and avoid walking through the better neighborhoods. I veered off and followed the faint trail. I prided myself in my tracking abilities. There were no visible tracks, but the trail shimmered from tiny pieces of broken glass. As I slowly walked through a trampled area of two-foot-tall weeds, studying the ground below, I saw the blatant sign of a hobo. It couldn't have been any better if it had been a perfect print of a worn-out boot with holes in the sole. On the side of the trail was everything I needed to see. Wedged in the grass was a shiny, empty bottle of Thunderbird wine! I had seen the bottle many times. The writing on the bottle said "20% Alcohol," and on the top was a big falcon-like bird with both wings proudly stretched from side to side.

This was it, the main hobo trail. I looked back toward where I had come and then up toward the direction I was going. Yep, a bum's secret highway. I walked a little further, scanning the ground for the perfect place to stash the quarters. Again, I didn't want it to be too obvious, but I felt it needed to be somewhat obfuscated. I didn't want it to be discovered by a hobo briskly heading up the trail like he was on a mission. I wanted it to be found by a bum who was walking slowly, looking at the ground, much like the way I walked.

A little further along, I saw a few pieces of broken concrete that someone had dumped on the vacant property. I walked over to it and imagined a tired hobo sitting there to rest on his weary trek. This was perfect. I stashed the quarters in the back, between the broken piles. I looked it over, gave an approving nod, and walked the twenty yards or so back to the little trail. I glanced back at the broken concrete. I pictured a hobo sitting there and then taking a swig from his brown paper bag. But then my mind saw him stand up and walk back toward the trail. Dang it! What if he didn't see the coins? I thought about it for a minute and then got busy on my hands and knees, picking up pieces of glass and small pebbles. Once I had as many as I could carry, I hustled back to the concrete. With one little piece at a time, I made an arrow pointing toward the quarters and spelled out the word "LOOK." It was perfect. Even a bleary-eyed half-drunk hobo couldn't miss it.

I skipped my way back toward town with the lightness of a fresh start. A hobo would get ten dollars, and I could re-devote my life to the straight and narrow path. I was sure God would forgive me. My mom never even believed me. And other than my accomplice, Sammy, not another person in the world would ever know of the heist.

A couple weeks later, I was back in town. My mom was buying groceries and then going by the post office. She let me amble off with the promise that I'd meet her at the post office in forty-five minutes. That was all the time I needed. Once I cleared her vision, I broke into a full-speed run. I needed to know that some fortunate hobo had picked up the quarters. I ran toward the packing sheds, cut over from the big tanks, and found the little trail toward the water tower. I never even slowed down until I skidded up to the broken concrete slabs, panting and out of breath. I looked down to see the broken glass and pebbles had been picked up and rearranged. I smiled to see the word "Thanks."

I can't say that from that day forward, I demonstrated nothing but an exemplary life. I was young. I had plenty of time to go on and break almost every remaining law of God and man at least once or twice. But stealing wasn't one of them.

Nope. That short-lived but painful burden was enough for a lifetime. I'd never again steal. But the whole sordid mess changed me even more. To this day, I will walk across two busy streets to put something in a homeless man's cup.

2

YOLO

Fifty years ago, my brother invented "YOLO" before it was ever a thing. You Only Live Once. When we were kids, he lived it. But he went a step further. He would think up some crazy idea. Then he'd follow up with, "Come on Rawge, we gotta do it! We ain't getting no younger!"

I'd look back at him with hesitancy, and think to myself, "Why would you say that? You're only eight! We've probably got time!"

But I missed the point.

It wasn't until I was grown and middle-aged that I really figured out what he was talking about. It wasn't about getting too old. It was about not being young enough. He knew way back then that if you did something dumb, or risky, or plain stupid, and got caught, you could slide by if you were young enough. Folks would say, "They're just kids. They just didn't know any better."

But at some unknown age, things would change. You could do the same thing, get caught, and end up in big trouble. "You're old enough! You should have known better!"

Steve knew that we weren't getting any younger and we needed to take full advantage of the youthful indiscretion clause before it played out.

Steve died during the Pandemic. I miss him. I've decided that when I get really old and people think I've lost my marbles, I'm going to pay homage to Steve. I will do stupid stuff and just listen to people say, "Leave him alone.

17

He's an old man and doesn't know any better."
I ain't getting any younger!

3

A Pigeon Named Homer

In California's Great Central Valley during the 1960s, most everyone was poor. There were varying degrees of poorness, but they all still fit nicely under any definition of the word. When my parents purchased anything, it was on a payment plan. New living room furniture, cars, appliances, and most anything else were touted less about the actual cost and more about how cheap they could make the payments.

"I can get you in that car for forty-six dollars a month!"

"You can take this refrigerator home today for just eleven dollars a month!"

Many times, I sat with a bored look on my face while my parents haggled with a salesman on the second floor of the Montgomery Wards building or in the parking lot of King's Auto. The question was always the same: How cheap can you make the payments?

We had a car, a refrigerator, and living room furniture, so at the end of the month, there were never many dollar bills left. As much as our economy has been built around the trickle-down factor, from the top to the bottom, the trickle-down from poor parents to poor kids was about zero. So, if I wanted a dollar or two in my pocket, it was up to me and my innate cleverness to get it.

In 1969, I was nine, and my little brother, Steve, was seven. I wasn't quite old enough yet to be expected to do much real work around the ranch. I spent my time taking care of my own stuff. I had a bunch of chickens, some ducks, and a loft full of pigeons. I loved the pigeons. I had every color from blue-gray to pure white. Some of them had pretty tufts on their heads and fancy feathers on their feet. A few of them were rollers that would tumble down through the sky, like they had died, only to catch themselves before they hit the ground and then fly back up to do it again. But most of them were just descendants of the boring gray, homing pigeon. These pigeons had an instinct that if taken away from their home roost, they could navigate through the air and get themselves back home.

One day I read how homing pigeons had been used during a war to secretly carry important messages between front-line soldiers and command posts. I decided to try and see if mine could do it. I knew that my mom was planning to drive into Huron, the closest town to our ranch, to do some shopping. I'd always go along and then bum around town while she shopped. So, just as she was inside getting ready, I ran out to my pigeon coop and got my biggest homing pigeon, which I'd so creatively named Homer, and brought him into my bedroom. I scribbled my name on a piece of paper and wrapped it around his leg. I gently placed a couple of rubber bands on it to keep it in place. Just as Momma hollered at me to get to the car, I carefully placed Homer into the Army Surplus knapsack that I carried with me almost everywhere I went. It was usually full of books and notepads, but on this day, it had live cargo. If I could just keep it quiet, we could get to town, and I could test his navigational skills.

I usually sat in the front seat, but it didn't seem to raise any hackles when I chose to sit in the back. I just pulled out a book and pretended to read while I had the other hand in the knapsack, consoling the pigeon. Within ten minutes, we were pulling into the parking lot of Ray's Market.

Momma told me that she was going to the post office after buying groceries. I was told to be there in forty-five minutes. I knew the drill well. I'd done it many times. As well as I hoped a pigeon could navigate without a compass, I had mastered the art of knowing the passage of forty-five minutes without the aid of a clock. I slid out of the car, looped the green bag over my shoulder, and headed for a vacant lot behind the store.

The lot was pretty well grown up with weeds, but there was a trail that cut across it from corner to corner. I walked to about the middle. Shielded by the weeds, I pulled the pigeon out of the bag. I held it for a minute and looked into its yellow-brown eyes.

"Good luck, Homer. Safe travels." I gave him a little toss into the air and let go. Within seconds he was flying in small circles and gaining altitude. A few seconds later, he disappeared east, at what seemed to me exactly the direction of our farm. I smiled. It might just work. His home was only about five miles away, but it was five miles that the pigeon had never seen before.

I was waiting at the post office as Mom pulled into the parking lot. I knew the combination to our little mailbox and was standing with a bunch of envelopes clinched in my hand.

I hopped in the car.

"Here, Mom, I already got our mail. I'm ready to get home. I need to get to the bathroom." I was anxious to get home, and the statement was true enough not to cause me any guilt. Mom pulled the car onto the road, and we headed home.

We pulled down our driveway and parked on the little parking spot outside our front door. It was the only piece of concrete on the whole farm. I hopped out, told Mom bye, and headed, at a run, for the pigeon coop.

Mom hollered, "I thought you had to get to the bathroom?"

I hollered back, "I'll do it out here!" and disappeared without looking back.

I walked up to the coop slowly, looking it over as I approached. A big smile hit my face as I saw Homer sitting in front of a wide wire door I had built for them to get in and out. I slowly pulled a rope that opened it, and Homer jumped in, anxious to get inside for food and water. I let the wire door close, then went into the coop through the regular door. I carefully snuck up and grabbed Homer. The note was still attached to his leg. I pulled off the rubber bands and sat him back down to eat and drink. I read the note: "Rawge Jones." My homing pigeon test was a success. Homer was a true homing pigeon.

I lay in bed that night, thinking about Homer. That was quite a feat. He had flown home, guided only by some mysterious pigeon ability. I wondered how far he could fly. How fast did he fly? What if he saw other pigeons on the way—would he fall in with them and not come home? I had questions. Maybe I'd try it again sometime.

A few weeks after the test flight, I was watching *Hopalong Cassidy* on TV. Hoppy was dealing with a bunch of scoundrel bank robbers who were somehow getting alerted each time the posse headed for their hideout. Hoppy made sure that no riders left town, but still, the robbers had been tipped off. I sprang up when Hoppy figured out that a man in town was sending the robbers messages tied to a homing pigeon's leg! Those scoundrels had harnessed the pigeon's ability and used it for bad. I wondered how I might use it for good. Next, I wondered how I might use it to make money. I needed a few dollar bills and Homer just might be the answer.

I thought through some possibilities, but nothing seemed to have merit. It's not like I could rent him out to the Army to send messages in battle. It'd be pretty hard to compete with the US Mail for sending letters. But there must be something. Hmmmmm. Wait a minute! I had an idea! But I'd need to do a little research.

The next day, I stood in front of a big map stapled to the wall in the ranch's shop. I had a piece of string and a tape measure. I stretched the string from the middle of the city of Lemoore straight to our farm. People call that straight-across distance "the way the crow flies." It's also the way the pigeon flies. I measured the string: eight inches. Next, I ran the string from the middle of Lemoore to Highway 198. Then west to the Avenal cut-off. Next, I stretched it over to Gayle Avenue, then west to our little road. I finished by stretching it the little drive to our house. I measured the string: nine and a half inches. I jotted the numbers down in my notebook. The scale on the map indicated that each inch equaled two miles.

I walked back to our house and sat down to do some math. Eight times two is sixteen miles. Nine and a half times two is nineteen miles. The route from Grandma and Papa's house to mine was three miles shorter for a pigeon than a car. Now I just needed to visit our treasured World Book Encyclopedia for the final details. I found a few notes about how fast various birds can fly, and fortunately, there were details about pigeons and their homing abilities. The article indicated that pigeons can average sixty miles per hour for short distances. That was about the same speed that a car can travel for most of the trip. The car would have to go even slower for the last half mile on our crappy dirt road. But that was all the information I needed. A pigeon could beat a car from Grandma and Papa's house to home in a race.

As I thought about a plan, my first thought was to challenge Dad to a race and put some money on it. I felt pretty strongly that he'd be sure he could beat a scrawny pigeon. But I knew he'd lose because he didn't have all of the highly detailed background information that I had put together. But as I thought it through, I worried that since it was a race, Dad might risk a speeding ticket and drive seventy miles per hour. Even with Homer flying at his top speed and taking the as-the-crow-flies shortcut, the race would be too close. I needed a sure thing!

I thought back to the genesis of the whole pigeon idea—the bank-robbing outlaws. They had been very secretive. The note-carrying pigeon was unknown to everyone except them. The pigeon secretly carried a note that reached the outlaws but was unknown to the sheriff's posse. Boom! I had a plan.

The only downside to my plan was that I'd need help from my brother Steve. I called him over to gauge his interest and abilities.

"Steve, I need your help with something. If you help me, there's probably a little money in it for you."

"How much?"

"I don't know. Maybe a dollar."

"Okay. What is it?"

"On Saturday, when Pops goes to Grandma and Papa's house for lunch, I'm gonna go with him, but I'll need you to stay here. After we're gone for a little while, I need you to sit in my pigeon coop and watch the roof. When the big gray pigeon that I call Homer lands on the roof, pull the rope and let him in. When he's in, grab him and look for a note that will be wrapped around his leg with a rubber band. Read the number on the note and memorize it. Then, be waiting for us to get home and then tell Dad that number. Don't say nothing else but that number. Don't say nothing about a pigeon. Just say that number. If you have to, you can say you got the number from the air. But that's it. Can you do it?"

"Yeah, that's easy. I'll do it."

I first used some wire and turned the inside of my knapsack into a portable pigeon transport cage. I wanted Homer to be as comfortable as possible. A few days later, I was sitting in Pop's pickup as we made the trip to Lemoore. We had made the drive many times. But this time, there was a gray pigeon, quietly and secretly, hiding in my knapsack. With crossed fingers, I launched my plan into action.

"Hey Dad, I've been reading about brain waves. You know anything about them?"

"No. Not really."

"I guess there's electrical currents in there and all kinds of stuff. I read that we only use about two percent of them. I read that there's all kinds of stuff that the brain might be able to do that we don't even know about."

"I know some people that use zero percent of their brains."

We laughed, and the plan was in motion. In fifteen minutes, I was in Papa's house, giving the customary hugs. While Pops ate lunch, I went out back to play. I took my knapsack cage and stashed it in the little shed between an old lawn mower and a box of empty Mason jars. I made sure Homer had water in a little hamster water tube hanging on the side. Now all I needed was to wait until Pops was ready to head back home.

When he finally walked outside, I was ready. I was sitting on his tailgate with my hands up, and fingers pressed against my temples.

"What the hell are you doing?"

"I'm trying to send Steve a message through the air."

"That's impossible."

"No, it's not."

"Yes, it is."

"No, it's not. You want to make a bet about it? Pick a number between one and one hundred, and I'll send it to Steve. I'll bet you five dollars that I can do it!"

"You don't have five dollars."

"I won't need it. I'll win."

"That's not how bets work. You have to back it up with money."

"Okay, I have three dollars at home. I'll bet you three dollars. Pick a number."

"One thousand and fifty."

"No, it has to be less than one hundred."

"If you can send a message, then it shouldn't matter the size of the number."

"Fine then. One thousand fifty."

I held my hands back to my temples, closed my eyes, and feigned concentration.

"Let's go, I gotta get back."

I hopped down and closed the tailgate.

"Oh wait! I forgot my knapsack!"

With that, I busted around the corner of the house before he could stop me. I ran to the shed, grabbed a pencil and paper from my bag, and started to write. I paused as I thought about the number. I suddenly wasn't sure that Steve would even know the number 1050. So I wrote it out – one thousand fifty. With fingers crossed, I attached it to Homer's leg and gently tossed him toward the sky. I watched as he quickly disappeared... in the wrong direction!

Oh no! What had gone wrong? Was he disoriented after spending an hour in the bag? Would he eventually get his wits and get back on the right path? How long would that take? Oh no! With a bunch of thoughts running through my mind, one that came to the front—I needed to stall for time.

I ran back around the house to the truck. The engine was running as I opened the door. I threw my knapsack into the seat but hollered to Dad that I hadn't given Grandma and Papa a goodbye hug. Before he could respond, I ran back to the house and disappeared behind the screen door. I gave them hugs and went back to the truck. I crawled into the seat and was met with the simple statement, "Close that damn door! I'm gonna be late."

As we drove west on Highway 198, I saw the big round speedometer behind the steering wheel. We were doing a little over sixty-five mph, but I'd hoped for a more leisurely sixty. I turned around in my seat and looked behind us.

"Is that a cop back there?"

Pops let off the gas pedal and looked in his rear-view mirror. "Only if they've switched over to driving red cars nowadays."

27

He gave me a disgusted look and put his foot back onto the pedal. A few minutes later, we left the highway and turned onto the Avenal cutoff. The cutoff was a two-lane road that stretched from Highway 198 to the small town of Avenal. We had gone about a mile when I squirmed in my seat and asked Dad to pull over and let me pee. He insisted that I could hold it until we got home. After only a couple minutes of me squirming and making high theater of my need for a break, he skidded the truck to the shoulder and gave me a loud "Hurry up!"

I slid out of the truck and walked to the back. I stood close enough to the tailgate that I doubted my head even showed in his rear-view mirror. As I pretended to pee, I looked up in the sky. As much as I'd hoped to see the flash of a gray pigeon whoosh by, I moved my gaze further into the heavens, hoping for a little luck to rain down.

I was startled by a loud honk from the front of the truck. Pop's always-thin patience had dwindled to nothing. "Let's go," he hollered.

I stood for another moment and then got back in the truck. There was nothing I could do now. It was up to Homer.

We turned off of Gale Avenue onto our dirt road. In just a couple of minutes, my scam would play out. I stared through the windshield as we wound through our little driveway, ringed by oleanders. At the last minute, I saw Steve sitting in the driveway. But Dad didn't pull in. He just stopped the truck and told me to get out, that he was in a hurry.

"No! We've got to check in with Steve! We've got a bet! I want to see if it worked."

"Damn it!"

Dad opened the door and got out. He motioned for Steve, who hopped to his feet and headed in our direction.

"What's on your mind?"

"One thousand fifty," Steve said through a grin.

"How do you know that?"

"One thousand fifty."

"Listen, no more bullshit. How do you know that?"

"One thousand fifty."

Dad stared at me for a minute. I knew the look, and I never liked it. It was dark. It was foreboding. But then he cracked a tiny bit of a smile and reached back for his billfold. He pulled out three one-dollar bills and handed them in my direction.

He shook his head and continued staring at me with his half-mad, half-curious smile.

"I guess you used the full two percent today."

Pops got back in the truck and drove off. I gave Steve a dollar and reiterated his vow of eternal secrecy. I watched Dad's truck disappear in the dust. It had worked. I knew Dad would dwell on it for a while, but he'd never figure it out. It was a perfect trick.

I also thought about it for a while. I went back and forth between it being a fun and innocent trick to fool my dad and it being as crooked as the scoundrel bank robbers fooling the sheriff. But it bothered me. I had managed to add another entry into my ever-growing guilty conscience. As much as I tried to err on the lighthearted side and forget about it, it gnawed at me.

A couple of weeks later, I met Pops coming into the house as I was walking out. We exchanged a couple of "Heys" in passing, but he put his hand on my shoulder and stopped me.

"Make sure you buy some good pigeon feed with that three dollars."

He had that half-angry and half-amused smile again. I just nodded with wide eyes.

I walked out to my pigeon coop and sat down. I couldn't write off Dad's sudden interest in my pigeon's health as a mere coincidence. He had figured it out. But how?

It hit me as I sat and listened to the cooing of a pen full of pigeons. Maybe there is such a thing as sending mind waves, and I have been sending guilty waves for a week! Pops had picked up on it! Well, no. I made that up. Sending brain waves is impossible.

But just in case, I vowed to think about nothing for the next week except how great and understanding my pops was! The thought may not have traveled through the air and into his mind, but it did manage to etch itself into mine.

It still jumps into my thoughts every once in a while. Pops was great!

4

Keep It Short, Rawge

I write short stories, but too often, my mind thinks of novels. Sometimes, it's difficult to keep my stories succinct. It's a struggle to keep my mind in the right space.

In short stories, the ending or moral is the focus, not necessarily the details. Finding the perfect balance of brevity and description is a challenge for any writer, even more so for me.

Here's an example of what I'm up against.

This is what I need to write:

It was cold outside, but I started walking down the lane to our mailbox. The icy wind made me change my mind.

But here's what I invariably start with:

Within five steps to the mailbox, I felt the icy wind hit my face. It's the wind that blows in from the north. I know it well. It travels over the snow and ice, up in the mountains for days, before dropping into our valley to bite my red nose and ears and turn my fingertips white. It's a wind so cold that it stings your lungs with every breath but leaves your throat numb and dry.

I turned my face away from the blowing cold as I pondered what could be sitting in the mailbox. My mind pictured letters, bills, and the assorted junk that's always addressed to the "box holder." During that brief thought, a big icy gust, even colder than before, hit me in the face.

Then there was my answer. It's just mail. It can wait until tomorrow.

Keep it short, Rawge! But long enough to call it a chapter!

5

Grace and Well-Chosen Words

When I was about seven years old, I went to a rodeo in Riverdale, California. Festus Haggen was there, walking around and greeting people. He was a side character in an old western series called *Gunsmoke*. Every ranch kid watched it. Festus dressed in his classic *Gunsmoke* garb consisting of a worn-out hat, shoddy black vest, a six-shooter, and boots with spurs. While the main characters, Sheriff Matt Dillon and the saloon operator, Miss Kitty, were a good-looking pair, Festus was the opposite. He had one crazy eye, walked with a bow-legged gait, and talked in a folksy drawl. Sheriff Dillon rode a beautiful buckskin horse while Festus rode a mule. But all that was what made him attractive. The wall-eyed Festus was my favorite character, so I walked around the rodeo grounds until I found him.

When I finally saw him, I just walked up to him with a big grin. He saw me, knelt down a little, cocked his crazy eye, and said, "Well howdy! Are you gonna be a cowboy someday?"

I lowered my eyebrows at such a ridiculous question.

"I'm a cowboy right now!" I snapped back with some tone in my voice.

It was only one second into the conversation, and he'd already made me mad. So I followed it up with, "How about you? You gonna be a cowboy someday?"

Festus stood up, reared back a bit, lowered his own eyebrows, and said,

"Well you're a feisty feller!"

Then he got a hint of a rusty smile and said, "If you ain't a cowboy, you sure act like one!"

The line won me over. I regained some of my seven-year-old composure and realized that I was in the presence of a bona fide Hollywood actor. I needed to show more respect. I apologized for my rude response to his innocent question.

He got a big grin and said, "Oh, it don't matter none! I could tell you was a cowboy the moment I laid eyes on you!"

We chatted a little more, and then he autographed my rodeo program. He wrote, "To the biggest cowboy I met in the whole town of Riverdale. Your friend, Ken Curtis."

Festus and I got off on the wrong foot, as I've done with many others countless times since then. It happens. But a few well-placed words and some grace turned it around. We parted, shaking hands, with smiles on our faces.

Grace and well-chosen words.

The
Pen is
Strong

6

Writers & Readers

Any writer wants to write a best-seller. But a book is more than just words. It's the correct words that connect with an audience. As much as we strive to put words on paper, we strive to understand our readers. I've learned that I'm not very good at it.

Suppose that I wrote the sentence, "The pen is strong."

A seven-year-old, just learning to read, would sound out the words and then wonder how a pen could be strong. It doesn't even have muscles. He'd wander off from the sentence and flex his muscles. "I'm strong. Look at my muscles, Mom!" He'd be lost.

A teenage girl would read the line and think about it. After a minute, she'd probably make some sense out of the metaphor. But a teenage boy would likely point out that the two words in the middle spell "penis" and then just laugh.

Twenty-somethings would think about it and then verify it by thinking about everything they've ever read that has moved them in some way.

Thirty-somethings and older have started to have their real-life kick in. So, they might read it and push back. They've got circumstances to bounce thoughts off of. They might question the premise based on something in their history. They'll think about it, and then move on, but it will leave something resting in their minds.

So, writers have a tough job as they try to direct readers to where they want them to be. It takes a lot of thought, an understanding of the human mind and the human condition, and work.

Writers often talk about the hours or days spent trying to get a sentence or paragraph worded just right. Writers love to talk about their successes and failures. I've spoken with many who remember a paragraph that they worked on so long, but it ultimately brought the whole story together. Others tell me about the paragraph they wish they could go back and change. It's work.

I want to send some kudos to those hardworking writers who sweat, cry, drink, and lament over their paragraphs before they ultimately move us with their words.

The pen is strong!

But dang it! Now I can't un-see the word *penis*. 🙂

7

Zen Morning

O ur farm grew cotton, barley, melons, and a few other crops. I occasionally got to see it all from the sky when I'd get a ride in a family friend's little airplane. The contrasting colors, coupled with the different patterns, were always pretty and interesting. The cotton fields were planted in perfect rows that ran east to west in every field. The barley fields had no rows and were just a square swath of green, framed by roads or irrigation ditches along every side. The melons were in rows. The alfalfa was open like the barley but had ditches scattered wherever my dad made them to allow for flood irrigation.

From the air, the whole sight was pretty. But if someone were looking at the same hodgepodge of colors and stripes and patterns on a woman's clothing, they would call it busy. I've heard my wife say it many times. She'd look over an outfit or even just a piece of fabric, step back, and say, "Too busy! Stripes, plaids, and solids are not okay. Stripes and solids, okay. Brown or white or just blue is even better."

I'm not one of those people who gets overly bothered by such things. I sleep just fine in a room with a picture on the wall that is hanging slightly skewed. I never feel the need to fix something that is slightly unbalanced. I don't even flinch when the gas pump clicks off at $49.99. But on occasion, I will see something as too busy. I confess, I have a fondness for the smooth and plain.

My favorite time on our farm was in early winter when every field had been plowed and disced. Just after the cotton had been picked, we used a tractor-drawn machine to cut the cotton stalks down to ground level. Then the big tractors pulled a disc and a roller at an angle across the rows, leaving nothing behind but smooth soil. At the same time, the barley fields that had been harvested were being disced and prepared for the planting of cotton next spring. So, for a few weeks, our entire two thousand acres was a homogenous palette of beautiful brown dirt.

I liked that time the best. It was somehow relaxing, somehow comforting. If Zen was onto something with the little sand garden and a rake, this was that calming feeling times two thousand acres. You didn't have to see it from the air. You could walk along the ground and feel it. You could look to the west and see brown dirt all the way to the horizon. You could see the same thing to the north, south, and east.

Every once in a blue moon, my dad would announce that he wanted to take us all on a trip. I was excited when he told me that we were driving to the ocean on Saturday. Pismo Beach was only about two hours away, but I had never been there. Seeing the ocean for the first time was on my bucket list fifty years before the "bucket list" became a thing. We would stay the night in a motel and get to swim in a real pool. We would see the ocean and splash around in its salty waters. We'd eat at a restaurant, and I might even get to eat shrimp. I was so excited.

My oldest sister, Paulette Hope, had already married and moved away. My other sister, Sharon Lynne, didn't want to go and would stay with a friend. The trip would just be Mom and Dad, my younger brother, Steve, and me. So, on Saturday morning, we loaded a single beat-up suitcase full of clothes and got on our way.

I stared out of the window for the entire drive from the San Joaquin Valley into the Coast Range mountains. I pointed out oak trees and patches of California poppies. I called out various birds and the occasional hawk soaring in the sky. Steve just pointed at cows.

Even without seeing the ocean, the drive would have been a vacation in itself. I reveled in any chance to see anything that wasn't our farm. But Steve could quickly take the fun out of a drive. I was ten, and he was eight. I wanted to watch the scenery, but Steve wanted nothing but to put his feet in my face and pinch me with his toes. I pushed them away and pushed them away, but he was relentless. I had already learned that it was pointless to try to ignore him. He liked getting me annoyed, but even without a reaction, he just genuinely liked having his feet on me. I knew better than to make a big commotion. Mom would turn around and tell us both to settle down. Dad would threaten to turn the car around, and Steve would just keep on being Steve. So I sat for two hours with my face to the window and Steve's grubby feet on my side.

As we got close, Dad told us to keep a watch toward the west. He announced that any minute, we would see the ocean. The west was on my side of the car. With Steve piled on top of me, I raised up as high as I could in the seat and watched. Just as Dad promised, we rounded a curve, and there it was—the Pacific Ocean!

From a distance, it was everything I thought it would be. It was blue and seemed to stretch forever into the horizon. I could look down and see the white breakers where it met the rocky shore. A little farther down the road, the shore turned to sand, and I could see people walking on the beach. A few more turns and it disappeared behind buildings. But I knew it was there. I could smell it!

Dad drove the car down some streets, straining to read the little street signs. Mom pointed with her finger and gave him directions. Before long, we pulled into the driveway of a motel. Dad stopped the car in front of the lobby and told us, "Wait here." I watched him disappear through a door and then reappear with a key attached to an orange plastic diamond with a big "14" on it.

Dad got back in the car, drove a hundred feet past a small swimming pool, and parked in front of room 14. I was proud when he handed me the key and told me to open the door while he got our stuff. I threw a prideful glare at Steve and hopped out of the car. In a minute, we were surveying the inside of our room. It had two beds, a little table with two chairs, and a bathroom. I thought it was perfect. Dad glanced around and then looked at Momma. "I guess it will do." Momma nodded.

Our suitcase was propped on a little folding stand. Steve threw it open and started rummaging for his swimsuit. He started yelling, "Let's get in the pool! Let's get in the pool!"

"No!" I countered loudly. "We're going to the ocean. We came to see the ocean!"

Mom jumped in, "Both of you, stop!" and she looked over to Dad.

It got quiet, and we all stared at Pops. He thought for a second. "No, let's walk down to the beach. You two can roll up your pants legs and wade in. You can get in the pool when we get back."

And that was that. I was about to stick my feet into the Pacific Ocean.

We walked as a family for a few blocks. I took the lead, with my head high, straining to see the water. Steve did what he always did and walked right behind me, deliberate steps on the heels of my shoes, trying to give me a "flat tire." Before a dozen steps, his toe caught the back of my tennis shoe and pulled it off.

"Stop that, you brat!" I yelled as I bent over to pull the shoe back over my heel.

"You two boys!" came in a loud voice. It was in unison. Mom and Dad had practiced it a million times, and I had heard it a million times. Steve would act like a brat. I would react. Then there it was, "You two boys." In trouble, we were always a pair.

I could hear waves and smell the ocean water. We rounded the corner of a building, and a long sandy beach spread out in front of us. A pier separated the beaches and extended well out into the ocean water.

I turned to Dad, "Can we get in?"

"Roll up your pants, and don't get in past your knees, or you'll drown."

We both started running through the sand at full speed.

"And watch for sharks!" Dad yelled.

I skidded to a stop and looked back. Dad laughed. "Just kidding. Go on."

It didn't take long for Steve and me to kick our shoes off, pull off our shirts, roll up our jeans, and walk onto the damp sand. We did what every person in the world does on their first time at the beach. We walked in the wet sand out toward the waves, then screamed and ran back, trying to outrun them. It was a game of dare to see who could wait the longest before running away.

Mom and Dad sat in the sand next to our shoes and kept an eye on us. At first, we did what we were told and only ventured in up to our knees. But as we got used to the cold, we were both soon in water up to our waists. But even with soaked pants, it was fun.

It seemed that we had hardly even been there when I saw Dad standing up and motioning for us. I waved in acknowledgment and grabbed Steve by the arm. He yanked his arm away and ran down the beach in the opposite direction. I looked back at Dad. He pointed a finger with the familiar gesture—go get him.

It would have been easier to chase down a wild dog. Steve ran through the sand and water in zig-zags with me behind him. I would get close, and he would spin and run in the opposite direction. We covered a hundred yards before he finally stopped to look back, and I grabbed him by the shoulders. With a firm grip, like I was squeezing a wild animal, I turned him so he could see Dad. He'd always argue with me, but he knew Dad meant business. In a minute, we were standing in front of him, dripping wet and covered in sand from head to toe.

Dad pointed toward a little outdoor shower hidden at the back edge of the beach and sidewalk.

"You two are a mess. Get in and clean yourselves off as much as you can. The water's probably a little warm."

We both stepped in and fought for the spot beneath the warm water. I watched the sand disappear into the drain at our feet. We stepped out and took turns drying off with the single towel that Mom had brought along. We both put our shoes and shirts back on and again looked almost presentable to the world. Our pants were wet but would dry soon enough in the hot sun.

As we began our walk back to the motel, I stopped to look back at the beach.

"Well, what did you think?" Dad asked.

"It was fun."

"But what did you think of the ocean and the beach?"

"It's okay. It's kind of busy, not what I thought it would be from books and pictures."

"What do you mean?"

"It's covered in footprints. Everywhere. There's not a single piece of just pretty sand."

Dad looked the beach over. The afternoon sun and tiny shadows highlighted every single footprint. Except for a small fringe at the water's edge, the entire beach was a pitted mess of tracks going in every direction.

"Yeah, there have been a lot of people there today."

"But that's okay, thanks for bringing us."

We got back to room 14 at the motel and got ready to get into the pool. I hated that both mine and Steve's swim shorts had the same little palm tree pattern. Surely Mom could have found something that showed I was older. I deserved sea horses. Steve deserved palm trees.

We walked to the pool area. I was happy to see it was deserted. As Mom was yelling to Steve to use the steps, Steve ran to the pool and jumped cannonball style. I looked at Mom and shook my head. Steve and I were both good swimmers, and Mom wasn't concerned with him drowning, but there were signs everywhere that plainly read, "NO JUMPING AND NO RUNNING ALLOWED."

I gracefully waded into the water like a debutante descending a spiral staircase at a ball. I stood in the shallow water for a moment. Dad announced that we had thirty minutes while he walked a few blocks to get us Chinese food. He looked at me and said, "I know. You want shrimp." I flashed a big smile. But mid-smile, I was drenched in water as Steve landed a cannonball almost on top of me.

I wiped the water from my eyes and yelled, "Stop doing that, you brat!" I looked up to see Dad staring down at us, shaking his head.

"You two have fun," and he walked off.

I turned to Steve and put my finger in his face. "Do not splash me again!"

He immediately used his cupped hand to splash water into my face and into my eyes. Then he did it again. And again. I swam away, but he followed me, splashing water at me as he swam. I dove underwater and turned to look for him so that I could swim away. But even underwater, there he was, his face only a foot from mine, blowing out bubbles.

For the next half-hour, he was everywhere I looked. "Hey, Rawge, pretend I'm a sea monster. Hey Rawge, race you to the other end. Hey Rawge, who can stay underwater the longest? Hey Rawge, watch this. Hey Rawge. Hey Rawge. Hey Rawge!"

I was happy when Dad returned with a big bag full of food. Besides a sandwich in the car, we hadn't eaten, and I was starving. Mom set the dinner on a little table near the pool. I had fried shrimp and rice. Steve had wontons that he called "one tons." We sat and ate while Mom and Dad talked about how much the dinner cost and the motel room bill. Steve ate his dumplings with a plastic fork, and after each bite, he reached over to pretend to steal a piece of my shrimp. I knew he was pretending because he hated shrimp. But still, he enjoyed the pestering act of pretending.

We took our time with dinner as the evening slowly turned dark.

"Okay, bedtime," Dad announced. Mom picked up our plates and cleaned off the table. Dad handed me the orange key, and I ran to door 14. I stood with the door open and elegantly waved my hand for my mom to enter.

"Entre madame."

"Why thank you, sir," Mom replied.

But before she could take a step, Steve raced through the door ahead of her and jumped onto the bed. Mom just shrugged.

Steve and I put on our pajamas. We crawled into the bed and pulled up the covers. Earlier, Dad had turned on the little air conditioner that stuck out of the wall below the window. It didn't seem possible for the summer, but the small room was cold. Mom pulled a thin blanket from the top of a closet and spread it over our bed. There was no TV in the room, so when Dad said goodnight and clicked off the light, the room went dark.

I lay in bed on my side, facing away from Steve. There was plenty of space to avoid him and enjoy some peace. I lay there in the quiet, reliving the day in my head. The ocean water, the sand, the sound of the waves, and the soft hum from the air conditioner were perfect. I would sleep well.

As I lay in the stillness, I felt a barely perceivable movement. Then another. And then another. It was Steve moving around ever so slowly. I waited to see if he would get comfortable and settle down. But then, in one quick movement, he did it. In a well-rehearsed blink of an eye, he had both of his icy feet pressed against the skin on my back.

Well, that was it. A whole day's worth of frustrations busted out of me. I screamed and hit him with my fist. I was still pounding him in the back when Dad got the light switched on and yelled, "You two boys!"

There it was again. In trouble, we were a pair.

I grabbed my pillow and snatched the top blanket off the bed.

"I WILL NOT SLEEP WITH HIM," I announced. "I'll sleep on the floor. Sometimes I hate him!"

The room got quiet. I had used the H-word.

I dragged the blanket to the far corner of the room, as far away from Steve as I could get. I lay back down and pulled the blanket over me. It was still silent when Dad clicked off the light. In the quiet and the dark, I thought about the H-word. I imagined that Steve probably did too. I drifted into sleep with a heavy mind and heart.

I was awakened from a deep sleep, with Dad's hand gently shaking my shoulder. I looked up in the dim light to see his finger pressed against his lips in the universal symbol to be quiet. As I wiped the sleep out of my eyes, he quietly whispered, "Come with me and bring that blanket. Here's your shoes."

I walked as silently as I could while Dad gently opened the front door. Outside, he helped me slip my shoes on while he leaned in and said, "There's something I want to show you."

Dad held my hand as we walked back toward the beach in the faint light of dawn. It was quiet. There were no cars or noises, and there didn't seem to be another soul in the world. The whole town was still asleep. We walked a few blocks until we were back at the beach. We sat on the last piece of sidewalk and put our feet on the sand. Dad pulled the blanket over my shoulders.

In a quiet voice, he pointed toward the water, "Look, it's different."

I turned my head and scanned across the water. It was different. It was amazing. There were orange hints of light reflected in the tops of every wave. I slowly looked closer, and the whole beach, as far as I could see in both directions, was beautiful and smooth. The bleached sand was now a beautiful dark brown. There was no trash. There were no footprints. There was nothing but smooth golden sand.

I looked up at Dad with grateful ten-year-old eyes.

"I want you to remember this for the rest of your life. Every day starts over. Every sunrise means a brand new day. Look at the beach. The tide came up last night and washed everything away. It's fresh and clean. It's new. It may be covered in tracks and trash by the end of the day. Who knows? But right now, it is new. Will you think about that at every sunrise, Rawge, and try to start everything new?"

"I will," I said.

We sat in silence for a few minutes as the beauty and thoughts sank in.

"We better get back before your mom and brother wake up and miss us."

We walked back to the motel in silence. When Dad opened the door, it was still dark inside. I used my feet to slip off my shoes and gently crawled into bed with Steve. His back was to me, so I wiggled over to him and shared his pillow. I slowly put my arm over him and very quietly whispered, "I love you."

The moment needed the L-word.

It was sunrise, and everything was brand new.

8

Foul-Mouths and Footballs

My daughter's six-year-old boy said the word *shit* in school. People freaked out. The teacher alerted the principal. The principal alerted my daughter, and then she alerted me. When she told me about it, I sensed that buried within her tone was the accusation that he heard it from me. Well, I will admit, the word is in my vocabulary. It might even be my go-to word for a number of occasions. But he did not hear it from me.

As a boy on our farm, we all had dirty mouths. It came with the territory. It was only a handful of the more mildly bad words. But they were regular. They were regular when we were talking to one another. But if any adult was involved, our language cleaned up quickly. If it was a parent, grandparent, teacher, or any man of the cloth, our language reached squeaky clean status. So, daughter, I have practice and a keen sense of when and when not. The kid didn't hear the bad word from me.

Back on the farm, there was a common problem that plagued most every farm kid. If there was a line, we wanted to bend it as far as we could. Every boundary needed pushing. Every rule needed a little bit of testing. Language lines fell into this category. Sometimes the bad language line was the ditch at the end of a melon patch.

To break the monotony of growing endless cycles of cotton and barley, year after year, my dad planted two and a half acres of watermelons every spring.

He grew the big dark rattlesnake patterned Cobb Gems. There were always a few yellow-meat varieties somewhere in the patch, but the majority of the field was devoted to the big Arkansas cross-breeds. These were grown from seeds he saved each year from his biggest and best melons. They were light green, striped, and almost as big as a bathtub.

From the day the field was planted, Pops would walk out into the patch every evening to watch them grow. First, the seeds germinated, and two shiny green leaves popped open to harvest the sun. Next, the patterned leaves started. They grew along the ever-reaching vines. By early summer, they grew so fast that I swear if you stood long enough, you could see them grow.

Once the vines had spread six feet in every direction, little white and yellow blooms would appear. It was the bees' job to make sure every flower got pollinated and would become a melon. Dad would have a beekeeper friend leave a few boxes of bees at the end of the field. The bees worked tirelessly gathering pollen from one flower and dropping it off at the next. Pops would plow a ditch around the field and keep it full of water to satiate the bees' working thirst.

There were nights when the little golfball-sized baby melons doubled in size. They grew and grew and grew. By the middle of summer, the patch was his pride and joy. The field yielded hundreds of giant watermelons, some as big as a hundred and seventy-five pounds. A small one was forty pounds. One-hundred-pounders were the norm.

As much as Dad loved his melon patch, my brother Steve and I hated it. Dad was the field boss and we were the workers. It started with planting. Every crop on our farm had mechanical planters except the watermelons. Steve and I were the planters. We crawled along each row on our hands and knees. At about every six feet, we scooped out a small hole in the ground, placed two seeds a few inches apart, then covered the seeds with a half-inch of the moist clay-loam soil. One hole after the other. Six feet apart. One half-inch deep. Dad showed up every hour or so to make sure that we were doing it correctly. Exactly.

Planting time wasn't unbearably hot, but it was still hot. We started at six o'clock in the morning wearing shirts and pants. But by noon, the shirts were off and tucked in our back pockets. Dad insisted that we wear hats to keep the sun off our faces. He said it caused nose skin cancer. I guess there was no such thing as back skin cancer.

The grueling work of crawling on your hands and knees was bad, but it was nothing compared to what was ahead. Dad didn't grow the melons for profit. In twenty years and thousands of melons, he never sold a single one. He grew them to give away. He gave a couple to anyone who showed up. He gave them away for parties. He gave them away for charity auctions. Every church in a thirty-mile radius ate watermelon at their Sunday evening socials. All you had to do was ask.

But not everyone asked. There were people who wanted a truckload at night when we were all asleep. But by summer, when the melons were ripe and the pollinating bees were out of business, the ditch surrounding the patch was again full of water. It was then a giant moat. You could not drive a truck anywhere except to the very end of the patch, closest to our house. Every melon had to be carried out of the field, one at a time. To make it even worse, you had to walk over a couple of rickety two-by-ten boards that served as a bridge.

Throughout spring and into the middle of summer, Steve and I switched from melon planters to melon weeders and finally to melon harvesters. On most every afternoon, we could hear Dad calling for us.

"Hey, boys! Come here a minute! Go out there and get Mr. Jenkins three or four good watermelons."

Dad would sit on the tailgate and talk with whoever was there while Steve and I walked across the bridge, carrying a wrinkled old blue tarp. Pops had already staked out his prize melons, and we knew better than to touch them, but every other melon was fair game. We had been taught how to examine the curly tendril at the base of the melon's stem to determine if it was at peak ripeness.

Beginning with the closest melons, we would find a ripe one, cut its stem, and then roll the behemoth onto the tarp. Steve would grab the front and I would grab the back. On "Go," Steve would hoist the tarp up and onto his shoulder, and I lifted the back with both arms. We carried the load back to the end of the field and then "walked the plank," as we called it, before setting the cargo gently at the waiting truck or car's trunk.

Dad would look it over. "Oh, that's a nice one. It must be eighty pounds! Good job, boys! Now hurry and get a couple more!"

This was our near-daily ritual.

My dad's brother, Uncle Charles, also took people to the patch. Thankfully, his boys carried their melons out. Somewhere during the years, my cousins laid hands on an old army surplus battle gurney with aluminum supports on both sides and pairs of comfortable handles. It was a game-changer! If the right combination of melons were chosen, even Steve and I could carry as many as three at a time.

That was our summer routine. I dreaded seeing a car coming down our dusty road. Who was it now? Mr. Simmons, Papa Kinley's neighbor? The Baptist preacher? A relative that we hadn't seen since the last melon season? It seemed endless.

But this isn't a story about melons. This is a story about farm boys pushing the limits of their foul mouths.

August was the hottest month in Huron, California. By noon, it was already a hundred degrees, and it just got worse from there.

One afternoon, Steve and I were sitting on some worn-out folding chairs under the only big shade tree on the whole ranch. It was a hundred yards from our house but just far enough that we had some privacy and could still see and mostly hear if our names were called.

We watched a car come down our dirt road and pull into our little driveway. A man got out and walked to the door and knocked. Dad was inside, taking his lunch break and probably watching a ball game. The door opened, and the man walked inside. We both silently prayed that it was only a salesman. We looked at each other. Maybe he's just here to sell some fertilizer. Maybe it's just purely business.

Five minutes later, our questions were answered. Dad stepped out of the house, cupped his hands to his mouth, and yelled, "Boys! Rawge, Steve! Come here a minute!"

We knew better than to drag our feet. We hopped up and headed that way.

"Boys, this is Father O'Reilly. He's having a church celebration, and he needs four or five big watermelons." We looked over and saw a man smiling back at us with a give-away white-fronted collar—a man of the cloth.

"Sure, Pops," I said, "Bring your car over by the ditch, Mr. O'Reilly. We'll get you loaded up." I pointed in the direction of the field and headed over to find the green army gurney.

Father O'Reilly drove his car over and parked beside the ditch. He opened the trunk of his Cadillac and sat above the bumper with one leg still on the ground.

Steve and I crossed the ditch and walked into the field. We walked just far enough to be out of earshot of the priest. In our typical country-boy fashion, we started complaining.

"This is some bull shit!" I told Steve.

I'll stop the quotes here. But our coarse language got worse with every trip into the field. It got worse and started even sooner before we passed the bridge over the ditch. It was our way of pushing the boundary. The bad language was a form of protest against child labor. To us, every bad word was rebellion.

We carried that last melon, a beautiful striped eighty-pounder, and dropped it off at Father O'Reilly's truck.

"There you go, sir. The last one. I bet they're gonna be delicious." I addressed him with the utmost respect. After all, this was a man of the cloth.

"Thank you, boys. I know that's a lot of hard work. I really appreciate it." He smiled at us. He had a big toothy smile.

"But you know, you boys should really watch that bad language. Those were some really disgusting words you were using out there when you thought no one could hear. I could hear it, and I know God could hear it. "

Steve and I both froze. I looked at Steve and saw unspoken words in his eyes. They were the exact words that were in my eyes – *Oh shit!*

All I could do was avert my eyes in shame and mutter a soft, "I'm sorry, sir. We'll clean it up. It won't happen again."

The Father bid us goodbye with a handshake and drove off. We watched until his car was on the paved road. We were safe. He wouldn't be telling Dad about our swearing and thank God, he won't tell Mom!

We ambled back to the shade tree and sat down. We were embarrassed and a bit ashamed. We vowed to do better. The dark solemness lasted fifteen minutes. We heard another ranch kid hollering in the distance and we were off. Everything forgotten.

One evening, a week later, we were all sitting in the living room around the TV. We heard the dogs barking, the universal signal that a car was pulling in.

"Go see who it is," Dad said in our general direction. The impending game of chicken between Steve and me to see who broke and went to the window could only last a second before Dad raised his voice to say it a second time. My eyes were locked on Steve's, and I could tell that he wasn't moving. So, I jumped up and went to the big dining room window. I parted the curtains.

"Oh no, it's that Cadillac again."

"Who is it?" Dad yelled in my direction.

"I think it's that priest again," I yelled back.

Pops got up from the couch, went to the front door, and walked outside. Steve and I both went to the window and watched through barely parted curtains as the two of them talked. We looked at each other with fear in our eyes. Father O'Reilly was surely, at this very moment, telling Dad about our foul and disrespecting words in the watermelon patch.

A slip of the tongue with even a slightly bad word would yield a whooping. The words we were using would probably lead to the death penalty. This was bad.

We watched for a couple of minutes through the slit in the curtain. And then it happened. Dad cupped his hands to his mouth, "Boys! Come out here."

We knew better than to stall, but we walked down the hall to the door, heads down like we were walking Death Row.

"Boys, Father O'Reilly wants to talk to you a minute."

Dad shook the priest's hand, said goodbye, and walked back inside.

We were confused. Did he rat us out? Somehow, based on his expression, I didn't think so.

"We sure had a good time at our banquet! The watermelons were perfect. I just wanted to thank you boys again for lugging those heavy things out to my car!" He said the words again through his toothy smile.

"Here, I brought you something."

He reached into his open car window and pulled out a brand-new leather football.

"I'm sure you boys play football."

"Oh yes, sir!" I said. "All the time."

"Well, good." He handed me the shiny brown ball.

"Thank you, sir!" Steve and I both said in unison.

"Oh, and one more thing. I didn't tell your dad about your swearing and won't tell your mom. But I'm going to need both of you to work on it. Can you do that?"

Again, we both answered in unison, "Yes, sir!"

We shook hands and watched the big Cadillac disappear up the road. As the tail lights turned onto the paved road, Steve and I stared at each other in a somber disbelief.

Steve grinned at me, "That O'Reilly fella is a pretty good guy."

I looked back with an even bigger grin, "He sure is!"

We stood again with a few moments of silence, taking it all in. We had dodged the bullet. We pushed a boundary until it broke. We should have gotten a whooping or, even worse, had our foul mouths washed out with a bar of soap. But we didn't. We got a new football instead.

I seized the moment to help Steve understand the lesson. He was two years younger than me. He relied on me to bring the concepts around until they landed.

"There was a big lesson here, Steve. I hope you got it."

"I did, Rawge."

We both looked back towards the road and then back at each other. After another moment, we both yelled in unison, "Let's go play some damn football!!!!"

It would take another lesson or two.

9

Who is the Smartest Person in the World?

"Hey Momma, who's the smartest person you know?"

"That's a tough one."

"Why?"

Mom was at the kitchen sink, doing the dishes. She rinsed her hands and turned around to face me. Her momma instincts told her this was one of those conversations that would require a little more attention.

"Because some people are smarter than others, in different ways. Your Uncle Herbert is smart and probably knows more about hay and hay balers than anyone. He knows cars and motors, too. Your dad knows everything about farming. Your granny can sew and re-upholster furniture and car seats. Different people have different strengths."

"I know, but who is the smartest?" I asked, as I emphasized and strung out the word *smartest*.

Momma put down her dish towel and sat across the table.

"I still can't answer. Sorry. Who's the smartest person you know?"

She had turned the tables, but the answer was easy for me.

"You, Momma!"

It caught her off guard, but the answer was easy. Mom knew everything and could do anything. I loved talking to her. My dad was great, and we talked a lot. But talking with Mom was different. She could talk deeper and broader than anyone I knew. She and I could talk about serious subjects. We could pose questions to talk about that really didn't have answers. We could talk about God and the universe. We could discuss feelings. Mom wasn't the person I went to and asked, "What is seven times one thousand one hundred and twenty?" Mom was the person that I went to and asked, "Why are there bad people in the world that kill other people? Why are there wars? Why are so many people poor, but there are so many rich people in the world?"

Mom was special, and we were close. She doted over my sisters, Paulette and Sharon. She brushed their hair and made them beautiful dresses. She dressed them up for parties, and they looked like beautiful dolls on school picture day. She held my brother Steve close and watched over his reckless ways. She tried to stay one step ahead of him and keep him out of trouble in school. But she saved the long, deep conversations for me.

I talked with Momma every day until I moved away. But even then, I phoned her every week without fail. Today, we live in an unlimited-calls-to-anywhere world. Most people nowadays can't remember the outrageous costs of calling someone out of town. The long-distance calls were expensive. But I called home. Every week.

Even when I was well-grown and lived a few hours away, at college, I called home. Momma was the voice that kept me going when things got tough. On most college quarters, I chose my classes so I could have Fridays free. After the last class on Thursday, I would jump in my old pickup truck and head for home. Many nights, I'd arrive after midnight, but Mom would be waiting up for me. On most of those nights, we'd still be sitting and talking at the kitchen table when the sun came up.

I saw a meme on social media recently that read something like this:

Just Because You Have a PhD or College Degree,
It Doesn't Mean You're Smart!

I don't know what drove someone to post it, but I disagreed. It actually does mean that you're smart. They don't just give those things away. But I hope that maybe what the person was trying to say was that you don't have to have a college degree to be smart. That I wholeheartedly agree with!

My mom was born on an Indian reservation near Waurika, Oklahoma. Today, that city is best known for its annual Diamondback Rattlesnake

Hunting Festival. But in 1933, there weren't much more than a couple of thousand people, and many of them were dirt-poor. Even today, the median income in the area is less than $24,000.

When Mom was still a baby, the government told everyone they'd have to pack up and leave but not to worry because "they'd be in touch." They never got in touch. My mom's dad, my grandfather, was in prison. So, my granny and her brother packed everyone up and headed for California.

Through the struggles of being poor and moving along continually, school wasn't much of an option. But Momma managed to get through seven grades. The handful of school years, along with every single experience in her difficult life, lived in her mind. Struggles enriched her. Challenges deepened her. Everything in life made her the person who a seven-year-old boy and then a thirty-year-old man looked up to.

For the person who posted about not needing a degree to be smart, I hope you see this.

With only seven years of scattered schooling, my Momma managed to become the smartest person I've ever known.

10

Born to Snarl

"Hey Rawge, come here. Fransisco was checking ditches last night and told me he saw a coyote run across the road in the headlights, and it was carrying a pup. This morning, I saw a pup laying on top of the ditch over by the tower in section 10. The momma may have left one."

"Oh, Dad, let's go catch it! I could raise it!"

"No, we need to wait and see if the momma goes back and gets it. We need to let nature be nature until we know. I'll keep an eye on it."

"But if it's not getting food, it'll die!"

"Well, like I said, I'll keep an eye on it. But you can make sure you've got a pen to put it in, just in case."

I spent the day converting my empty chicken pen into a coyote pup pen. We still had an abundance of chickens from my gambling winnings and entrepreneurial venture, but I was an early adopter of the free-range concept. I encouraged the chicks to learn how to fend for themselves. So their empty pen would be perfect. The little pen was about six feet by six feet and was under the shade of a big paulownia tree. The wire was tight enough to keep chicks in, so holding a coyote pup wouldn't be a problem. I walked around our farmyard until I found some bowls suitable for food and water. I found a wooden box that someone had used for rabbits. It had a small entry door cut into the front, that was just the perfect size for a baby coyote. I put the box in one corner of the pen and loaded it with a couple of old burlap sacks. It wouldn't have a momma to sleep with, so it needed something to help stay warm.

It was a long wait. Ranch emergencies were a near-daily event and Dad didn't come home for lunch. It was late evening when he finally parked his blue Chevy pickup in the dirt beside our house. I was standing there waiting for him.

"Did you get it?"

"No, not yet. But it's still there. We need to give its momma a night to see what she's gonna do. If it's still there tomorrow, we'll go see if we can catch it."

I knew better than to argue much. But I was sure it would starve to death overnight or get eaten by something bigger. But maybe not. Maybe it would have enough wild sense to crawl back into its burrow and sleep.

That night I fell asleep thinking of what I would name it. I was a young avid reader, so I first thought of cool writer names like Bark Twain. Naw. Maybe another cool name-play like Snarl Marx. Naw. As names swirled around in my head, I decided I had better wait. I didn't even know if it was a boy or a girl.

Dad was up and out before the sun came up. It was the last Sunday in May and I had school the next day. I knew that if anything was going to happen, it needed to be today. I busied myself with my handful of weekend chores. I fed the horses, checked their water, fed our only dog, Jeremiah, and tackled a few other mundane tasks. But with every step, I looked up the road for dust to signal that someone was headed our way.

It was well before noon when I saw Dad pulling into his dirt parking spot. I ran and got to the truck before he could even put it in park. Pops got out holding a cardboard box with the top folded and sealed.

"Well, the momma left it so I got it. But it's wild and mean, and IT WILL BITE YOU. I brought you some welding gloves to handle it. DO NOT let it bite you. All I need is for you to get rabies or something and die. You hear me?"

"Yes, yes, I'll be careful. I promise."

"I think it's probably old enough to eat solid food. I'm sure the dog won't

66

mind sharing a little. Oh, and it's covered in fleas. Your papa sent you this powder that he uses on his dogs. Just sprinkle some on it, but don't get it in your eyes."

And just like that, I was about to try to save a little abandoned coyote's life. To ensure my success, I received some solid guidance—don't let it bite you, and don't get flea powder in your eyes. I was set.

I got the little box through the skinny door on the converted chicken pen. I set it down and cracked open the flaps to get a look inside. It was dark as I peeked through the crack. Staring back at me was the scaredest, and scariest, skinny bundle of hair I had ever seen. I snapped the box closed and put on the welding gloves. They were way too big for my little arms, and the thick leather extended almost all the way up to my armpits. I got my skinny fingers into the correct holes and squeezed a few times. The leather was stiff, but it seemed that I could make a grip if I was careful.

I opened the box, reached in, and grabbed the little animal by the scruff of the neck. I had handled enough animals to know that if I got it just right, I could hold it without it being able to bite me. The hold felt solid, so I lifted it out of the box and into the light. It growled and snarled and wiggled, but I held on tightly. I could see fleas crawling around the bare skin on its belly. I grabbed the cardboard container of flea powder and carefully sprinkled it until the animal seemed coated in it. I sat down in a corner of the pen and got ready to turn it loose.

The moment it realized it was free, it ran across the fence and bounced off the wire. It tried to get through the fence a few more times and then disappeared into the hole in the wooden box. I sat there for a while, hoping it would venture back out, but it didn't move. I didn't even hear a sound coming from the box.

After my legs were about to go to sleep, I stood up and made sure the skinny thing had everything it needed. I had set up a bowl of water and a bowl of dry dog food with a little water in it to soften it up. I knew that the first night would be the test. If it would come out of the box and eat some food, it might have a chance. I closed the door and checked it to make sure it was tight. "Goodnight, little coyote. I'll see you in the morning."

I fell asleep again thinking about names. My brief inspection had shown me that the coyote was a boy. The grimace on its face showed me that funny names wouldn't do, it needed a tough name. Names rolled around my head until I heard the name "Fang." That was it. Tough. Short. Bold.

The next morning, I got ready for school as quickly as I could. The moment I had my teeth brushed and enough clothes on, I ran out to the pen. It was barely daylight. As I rounded the corner of our yard, I saw Fang dash into the wooden box. I walked the last few steps slowly, just hoping that he had eaten some food. I was elated to see that the food bowl was entirely empty and much of the water was missing. I looked the pen over and could see that he had already worn the soil down along each edge of the wire fence. I was sure he had paced around the fence all night. I had seen caged animals do it at the zoo. It made me sad, but at least he had eaten.

"Fang, I'm sorry that you have to be in a cage. Just keep eating and growing for a few months, and then you can go free. I promise."

I spent every day after school sitting in the pen. I would shake the wooden box a little until Fang ran out, and then I'd cover the hole with a piece of wood. I wanted him to be outside. I wanted to see him. Watch him. At first, he would run to the opposite corner and push against the fence. But after a week or so, he calmed down. He wouldn't run to me and lick my face like a puppy, but he would walk around the pen, sniffing at the ground. Occasionally, he'd walk close and step over my outstretched legs. Once, he came along the fence and poked his nose between my back and the fence. I leaned forward just enough that he could squeeze through and come out the other side. That circle became a game. He would squeeze behind my back, pass through, then walk around the pen and do it again.

A few Saturdays later, I was sitting in the pen as the sun went down. My brother, Steve, was at a friend's house, and my folks were out for the evening. It was just me and Fang. On a whim, I cupped my hands around my mouth, tilted my head back and let out my best rendition of a coyote howl. I had heard them many times, and at my young age, I could hit some high notes. In fact, at that age, all I had was high notes.

Fang was a little startled at the sudden noise. But it felt fun, so I did it again but held it out a little longer. On my third try, Fang startled me! He jumped in to help. The little thing put his head back and howled louder than me. He followed my lead a few times, and then he took the lead. I felt like some kind of wild man, howling with a wild coyote. We howled for about fifteen minutes until I was too hoarse to try again.

Howling became our evening ritual. It was loud, and I'm sure Mom and Dad weren't thrilled about their son howling with a coyote. Even my brother Steve got in on it a few times. He could howl even better than me. He didn't get as much enjoyment out of it as we did, but it was nice to have the human company.

One afternoon, as I sat in the pen and Fang made his circles behind my back, he cut the corner and walked to my knee. He laid down and put his chin on my leg. It seemed like a sweet gesture, and I thought he might have turned the corner on some of his wildness. Instinctively, I reached over and put my hand on his shoulder, like someone might do to a tired puppy. But it was a mistake! In less than the blink of an eye, the wild animal snapped his head, sliced on my fingers, and stood frozen, staring at me with the fiercest grimace on his face that I'd ever seen. I snatched my hand back and squeezed my bleeding fingers.

He didn't run. Rather, he stood there staring into my eyes, with lips raised and showing every tooth and fang in his mouth. Even in my pain, I couldn't help but marvel at the visual power of his toothy glare. In less than a heartbeat, his face had gone from cute and cuddly to a look that would scare any man or beast.

It was perfect. Every tendon and muscle was placed in the perfect place to raise the lips and show the teeth. The muscles located above the canine teeth held that part up even higher, exposing the long fangs for everyone and everything to see. Other muscles lowered the eyelids and eyebrows to protect the eyes but gave them a fierce appearance in the process. The sudden tightening of all the facial muscles would instantly trigger the saliva glands. Within a second, the animal would drool, adding to the viciousness of the scene and deepening the guttural sounds of the growl. The whole show couldn't be better.

As I sat there, still squeezing my bloody fingers, the little canid backed up a few steps, looked away, and then every bit of the viciousness melted from his face. He no longer felt threatened and no longer needed the scary face. A few seconds later, he was right back to looking like a cute puppy. But he would never again be a cute puppy to me. I had learned a painful but very valuable lesson. I could look but not touch.

I walked out of the pen and washed my fingers with the garden hose. The water stung, but I could get a good look at the damage. It wasn't horrible, but the tiny little teeth had cut me like a dozen little razors. I shook my head and wondered how long it would be until I was stark raving mad from rabies. I shook my head as I remembered what my dad said the day he handed me the cardboard box with two pieces of advice. "Do not let it bite you" was already an epic fail. I grinned for a second and thought I might as well just squirt flea powder into my eyes and get it over with.

Over the next months, the little coyote grew quickly. I continued to howl with it every day. On some days, I could howl from the road as I walked home from the bus stop and hear him howling back. When I showed up after school each day with a can full of dog food, he would stand a few feet away, wiggle, and wait for me to fill up his bowl. There were days that he even wagged his tail. But I never again touched him.

By the middle of summer vacation, Fang was about half-grown. He was a little bigger than a Jack Russell terrier and had started digging holes around the sides of the pen. He wanted out. He wasn't grown, but he could surely take care of himself. I'd miss him, but he needed to be let go.

One afternoon, I opened the gate and stepped to the side. My half-grown coyote friend looked at the hole, took a couple of steps closer, and then bolted. I watched, just knowing that he would stop, look back longingly, and then feel the call of the wild. But no. Fang ran across our yard, through our pasture, and disappeared without even slowing down.

I stood by the door with a hurt look on my face. I waited ten or fifteen minutes, hoping he would trot back for a more meaningful goodbye. But there was nothing. I filled up his water and food bowls and left the door open. I figured he could probably avoid being eaten or shot, but I doubted he knew how to chase down a jackrabbit or pounce on a mouse. I'd continue to leave food for him, just in case.

For the next couple of weeks, the food was gone each morning. I'd howl in the evening, and he'd howl back, sometimes a half mile away. My dad treated it like a parlor trick. When he had friends over, he'd have me howl, and they'd all laugh when Fang howled back from some distant part of the farm.

After a few weeks, I decided that he could fend for himself. I didn't put food in the pen, and I closed and wired the door. That night I found out that he could fend for himself. My only white goose disappeared. And then a favorite chicken. And then another. And then another.

But I couldn't complain. I had wanted him to be a wild coyote and he was answering the call of the wild. Before long, he had thinned out the flock of chickens that weren't smart enough to roost in trees. The fat goose never really had a chance. Within a month or so, no more animals disappeared.

After school started, I took my evening shower, put on my bed clothes, and stood in front of the bathroom mirror. As young men often do, I leaned in and studied my face. As I did, I recalled the day I stared into the face of a scared wild animal and marveled at how perfectly it was created for a single fierce purpose. I did my best to curl up my lips and growl. It was bad. I tried again. I lifted one side of my lips and then the other. I squinted my eyes and tried again. No matter how hard I tried to produce a fearful grimace, I produced nothing more than an embarrassing and shameful fakeness.

And then I laughed at myself. I laughed until the chuckles faded into just a smile. And at that moment, something life-changing struck me no less than if a light bulb had appeared above my head. My face was not designed to growl. My face had a completely different purpose. The muscles, tendons, and attachment points on my face were designed for one purpose—to laugh and to smile! Yes! To laugh and to smile!

I kept a little journal in a notebook beside my bed. I scribbled stuff in it from time to time and drew pictures when I was bored. I mostly wrote stupid boyhood stuff, but that night, I wanted to remember something. I wrote a question and an answer.

Question: What if every person in the whole wide world only used their faces to do what they were intended to do and smile?

Answer: Everyone in the whole wide world would be happy!

11

Not a Lick of Common Sense

"**H**e ain't got a lick of common sense!"
I've heard it many times and said it almost as many times. Common sense is too often an element in short supply. Perhaps as science continues to explore and learn more about the human genome, we'll discover the common sense gene. Then we could say it's not their fault. It's just genetic, and they're missing the common sense gene.

I don't think it's genetic. I think we are all born with zero common sense. Then, as we age, we slowly develop it through trial and error, hap and mishap, and if we live through it, we end up with a nice pool of it to keep us out of trouble.

I wish that it was something easily measurable. If there was a standard test for common sense and we could each get a number, then we could graph it and watch how it grows over time. That's the scientist in me. Unfortunately, there's no test and no quantitative data. But, after sixty-four years of observation, I've developed some qualitative data based on my own empirical observations. I know it sounds pretty darn sciency! Here's what I've come up with.

We are all born with zero. Girls begin accumulating it at birth. With each passing year, their common sense goes up rapidly. By the time they are teenagers, they've accumulated a usable reservoir. It starts rising even quicker when they reach their early twenties and rises even faster once they reach their thirties.

Boys, on the other hand, are quite different. They are born with zero and accumulate it at the slowest possible rate. By the time they are seven or eight years old, they've *almost* accumulated a measurable amount. That tiny bit is almost enough to tell their brains, *that's fire, don't stick your fingers in it.* Almost enough.

I've noticed a peculiar change in the boy's growth curve at about 13 years old. At that point, everything they have gained (as little as it may be) is lost, and they start over at zero. It tends to stay at near zero until they are in their late 20s or early 30s. I've floated this hypothesis to many others to get their input. So far, I've received very few arguments. With this in mind, we must keep a close eye on our kids, especially the boys. Those kids ain't got no common sense! Childhood can be dangerous.

My childhood was perfect. I managed to keep away from girls and surround myself only with other boys who thought just like me. Very little was out of bounds. There was no criticism for making dumb mistakes. More importantly, there was a general attitude of "if it doesn't kill you, it just makes you stronger."

Oh, the good ol' days! I was eleven years old, strolling the tables of junk at the Monday Sale, a flea market in Hanford, California. Most every space had a table or two full of junk and then a ton of used clothes piled on tarps on the ground. I could look a space over in about five seconds and determine that there was nothing for me. I had a few dollars, and I certainly wasn't going to spend it on a used pair of Sears and Roebuck jeans or a wrinkled-up tee shirt.

As I passed from booth to booth, something finally caught my eye—a bow and arrow. I picked it up and took a look. It was beautiful. It was made of fiberglass with green streaks flowing through the whole curved bow. I had made many bows from limbs around our place but never had a *real* bow. As I looked it over, I asked the guy how much. He responded with three dollars. I asked about arrows. He told me it came with one arrow.

I had three dollars. I wanted to just buy it, but I had a tiny sense that this might be something I needed to clear with my dad first. I quickly asked the guy to hold it and I took off at a run to find Dad. I ran as fast as I could for two or three rows and then skidded up to him. I was panting, but I managed to get out the question.

"I have three dollars. Can I buy a bow and arrow?"

Dad thought for a minute. "I guess. You won't shoot your brother with it, will you?"

"Of course not! Thanks, Dad!" And off I went, hoping the beautiful bow was still there.

Once I handed the guy the three dollars, he showed me how to attach and release the bow string. He told me to keep it unstrung when not in use. He briefly showed me how to hold it and nock the single arrow and how to properly hold the arrow and string to make the pull. As a bonus, he gave me a little quiver to hold the arrow. As he was spewing off a final few safety tips, I cut him off with a quick "thank you" and started back toward the car. As I walked through the crowds of people, I pulled the bow over my head so that it lay across my back and did the same for my quiver and arrow. Since I had a bow and arrow and had to be around people where I couldn't shoot it, I at least wanted to walk around looking like a contemporary Robin Hood!

Once I got home, my dad reiterated his only bow and arrow rule. "Listen, Robin Hood, I better not see an apple on your brother's head. Got it? DO NOT shoot your brother."

I just laughed and assured him I'd be careful. Then, I got busy practicing. I was sure I'd be an expert in no time at all. I dragged a few hay bales from our feed room and stacked them in front of our barn. At least if I missed, the barn would stop my only arrow. I rummaged around until I found a cardboard box and drew a target on it with concentrically smaller circles, culminating with a nice bullseye in the middle.

I walked back about fifty steps, drew the bow, and took aim, just like the guy had shown me. My first shot wasn't even close. But the good news is that no one could ever tell that I was so bad. I couldn't hit the broad side of a barn. My arrow missed the target by several feet and bounced off the hard side of the barn. No worries, I've got the whole rest of the day.

After I walked back and forth to the barn about fifty times to retrieve my only arrow, I came to the realization that anyone who was any good at it probably had a whole stack of arrows. To make it worse, after about an hour, my arrow bounced off the barn, and I lost sight of it. It was lost in grass and dirt and weeds. In a panic, I walked side to side until I had covered the entire area. Then I did it again. After about fifteen minutes, I found it, well away from where I had expected.

I couldn't let that happen again. So, I walked to our big tractor shop and prowled around until I found a near-empty can of bright red International Harvester spray paint. I took it back to the barn and painted my arrow red. I used what was left in the can to paint my bullseye red. I finished by setting the spray can on top of the hay bales, just above the target. I knew it would be cool if I could hit the can and make it explode.

I walked back to my shooting area and nocked the red arrow. I drew the bow and aimed for the can. I watched the bright red projectile fly straight toward the target. Boom! A perfect bullseye! I was aiming at the can, but it fell three feet low and hit the bullseye. It was my first bullseye, so I took it as a win. It was an errant score, but I deduced that maybe I was aiming too low. I tried again, aimed high, and again, at least hit the target.

As I was nocking another arrow, my younger brother Steve walked up.

"Whatcha doin'?" he asked.

I didn't answer. It was obvious what I was doing. I just gave him a glare.

"Have you tried shooting blindfolded?"

Again, I didn't respond.

"Well, you don't know what you're missing. Get it? You're blindfolded, so you don't know what you're missing!" He laughed.

I just ignored him, and he ambled off towards the other farmhouses to join our cousins for some playtime.

My right arm was getting sore from pulling back the thirty-five-pound draw on the bow. My left wrist was beet red from the bowstring hitting it at each release, and my feet were tired from constantly having to walk a hundred feet or more to retrieve the single arrow. I unstrung the bow as I was instructed and placed it next to the target. I hid the arrow under the hay bales and called it a day. I'd keep trying, and I'd surely get better.

During the next weeks, I continued to practice. I had spent all of my money, so buying additional arrows was out of reach. I tried making some practice arrows but found that it's far more difficult than just scraping some bark off some straight twigs. A few of them actually shot, but my bad aim, coupled with the screwball flight of a crooked arrow, was dangerous to anyone or anything in the area. So, I plodded on with my one bright red arrow.

One afternoon I was driving around the ranch with my dad. We rounded a dirt road turn at the last of a half-mile row of big walnut trees. Just as we turned, a bunch of ground squirrels scattered and scrambled to dive back into the safety of their burrows.

"Damn squirrels! We'll never get a single walnut! How come you hadn't killed them all with that bow and arrow?"

Pops seemed serious. I was so busy shooting at a red splotch of paint on a cardboard box that I had never entertained the idea of hunting game. I had been told from birth that you don't shoot anything that you're not willing and ready to eat. I certainly wasn't going to clean and eat a nasty ground squirrel, but I suspected that the rule didn't apply to varmints. We didn't have a list of varmints, but just from hearing grown men talk, I had a sense that it included coyotes, crows, rats, mice, and thieves. And now ground squirrels.

The rest of the drive home, I plotted my hunt. I drew from the countless stories I'd read in the *Field and Stream* magazines. I recalled from books I had read how the famous man-eating tiger hunter, Jim Corbet, had carefully planned every step as he stalked his dangerous prey. I was about to turn a bunch of book and magazine reading into practical use.

It didn't take long before I had it all worked out. I would walk a half-mile down a little dirt landing strip between two cotton fields. At the end, I would skirt the edge of the field and use the two-foot tall cotton as cover. I would hunker low and slow, edging my way up to the walnut tree. I saw myself picking up a handful of dust and slowly letting it sift through my fingers to see which direction the wind was blowing. I would approach ever so carefully from downwind, only to step out at the last minute and let my arrow fly. I saw myself then walking over to the wriggling animal lying dead on the ground, with my signature red arrow sticking out of it. I'd shake my head and say,

"That's what happens to walnut-thieving varmints!"

I gathered up my equipment, took a big drink of water from a garden hose, and set off on my hunt. I knew it would take ten minutes or so to walk the half-mile to the end of the airstrip, so I put my bow and quiver over my shoulder, Robin Hood style. I had covered about half the distance when I heard a familiar sound.

Cawwww cawwww.

I looked ahead and saw a crow coming straight in my direction. I didn't see them often, but I had just recently decided that they were on the varmint list. I scrambled to get my bow and arrow off my body, ready to take aim. I hadn't practiced this maneuver and had not realized that the speed between a bow on my back and a bow in drawing position would ever be a matter of life and death.

As slow as I was, I got it into position just as the crow was almost directly overhead. I watched the red arrow go straight up, well behind the speeding crow, and then almost stop in mid-air. I watched it fall backward a foot or two and then head straight down and straight at me! I didn't understand much about gravity and the speed of aerodynamic falling objects, but before I could blink, it seemed to be coming at me even faster than it went up. I jumped a few feet over just ahead of the speeding arrow. I stood there with a pounding heart and looked down to see the arrow stuck in the ground at precisely the spot where I had been standing. Damn, Rawge!

I lost all thoughts of a crow or a squirrel. I'd almost shot myself with my own arrow. I could just imagine my poor momma having to hear the news:

"Rawge has been killed."

"What happened to him?"

"He accidentally shot himself in the head with his own bow and arrow."

After I thought it through a bit, and since I now had one arrow's worth of experience, I decided to try it again. I again aimed straight up, but this time only pulled the bow back to half-draw. The arrow would go less distance and presumably a little slower. The red arrow went up, turned around, and came back down. This time, I kept my eye on it and walked a few steps away to watch it hit the ground. I did it again. And again. And again.

After a bit of practice, I had it figured out. If I held the bow exactly perpendicular to the Earth, the arrow went straight up and straight back down. If I were off just a degree or so, the arrow would plunge back further away. Soon, I was bravely shooting it straight up and then only moving enough to let it hit as close to me as possible. It was now a game. As I walked home, I'd stop every thirty steps or so and shoot the arrow up. It seemed innocent. The red arrow was easy to see. It was fun.

A few weeks later, I was bumming around the ranch with my brother Steve, a couple of twin brother cousins, Bruce and Bryan, my best friend Montie, and a few other kids. It was a typical Saturday, throwing rocks at each other, climbing up on anything we could find, throwing some more rocks, and then sitting and complaining that there was nothing to do. Our ranch was two thousand acres with horses, cows, goats, chickens, trees, haystacks, tractors, bicycles, ditches, bee boxes, and more stacks of wooden pallets than you could count. But occasionally, even with the collective imagination of a pack of young boys, you could hit the wall. Bored with nothing to do.

In the midst of our gloom, I had an idea. "Go to the back of the boneyard and wait for me. I'll be right back. Stay low, and don't let anyone see you!" I gave the command and ran for my house.

The boneyard was the name of the area on the farm that collected everything that wasn't being used. There were farm implements, old trucks with the hoods up, and just enough ten-foot-high cotton trailers to hide the back of it from view. The tall cotton on the surrounding sides gave it the perfect amount of privacy for a bunch of near-senseless boys to develop new games. I was about to introduce them all to a game called "Dodge the Red Arrow."

In a matter of minutes, I crawled between two cotton trailers with my bow and quiver proudly slung on my back. I motioned for all of them to stand to the side, be quiet and watch. I put the arrow to the bow, drew it back, pointed to the sky, and let it go. Just as I had practiced, I watched the arrow peak and turn around, let my mind do its mental geometry to determine its landing spot, and then take a few steps to watch it hit the ground, a mere few feet from where I stood.

There were awes of admiration from my friends. I repeated it one more time to make sure everyone understood the game. Then I asked, "Who's first?"

My brother Steve had more nerve than any of us, so he marched right over. Giving him credit for his nerve is just a kinder way of saying that he was actually just a little crazier than the rest of us. He stood beside me and signaled that he was ready. I shot the arrow, and we both watched it fly. Steve stepped a handful of steps away, and the arrow hit the ground ten feet from him. Not bad for a beginner.

One by one, everyone took a turn or two. But just like any game, before long, we lost interest. We all went over to a stack of pallets and sat down. We talked and laughed and joked around. Someone ran to the shop and came back with a jug of water. We all took a drink and then continued our rousing stupid farm boy conversations. We had been sitting around for an hour or more when someone suggested we try the arrow game again. But this time, we all stand together and then run from the arrow.

The new wrinkle to the game seemed no more dangerous than the previous version, so I grabbed my bow. We all gathered in close, and I shot the arrow straight up with as much force as I could put on the bow. The red arrow disappeared into the sky. Something had changed. We had sat around for long enough that it was now noon, and the sun was straight above our heads. None of us could see the arrow. We all ran for cover, screaming as we went. As I ran, I squinted and searched the sky for the arrow. I had no idea if I was running into it or away from it. A few more steps and I spotted the red color heading straight down, a safe distance away from me. I skidded to a stop and watched it fall... straight into and out of my brother's head.

The group fell silent. I watched Steve fall to his knees and start crying. The whole group let out a collective farm boy, "OH SHIT," and ran over to Steve. He stayed on his knees, holding the side of his head with his palm. I could see blood on his hand.

I was silent. Pops had let me have a bow and arrow, with only one rule. "DON'T SHOOT YOUR BROTHER IN THE HEAD!" As ridiculous as it seemed at the time, I stood there looking at my brother with a bloody arrow wound on the side of his head and my red arrow sticking in the ground below him.

As we all stood there dumbfounded, apparently intent on letting my little brother bleed to death, my best friend Montie took the lead. He was undoubtedly the only one paying attention at Cub Scouts during the first-aid week.

He started screaming orders. "Here, give me your shirt!" he said, pointing at one of my cousins.

Cuz yanked the shirt off and handed it to Montie.

"Steve, hold this tight against your head!"

He handed the shirt to Steve's outstretched hand. Steve pressed the shirt against his head.

"The rest of you get out of here and don't tell anyone! No one! Got it?"

Every boy scattered, not wanting to be any part of this calamity.

We got Steve up and moved over to sit on a palette in the shade. After a few minutes, he quit crying. He said it hurt, but not as bad. After a few more minutes, Montie took a look. He slowly peeled the shirt away. It wasn't as bad as I had feared. There were two gashes on his head, and they had mostly stopped bleeding. Montie told him to put the shirt back on his head for a few more minutes.

We talked about what had happened in somber tones. I did my best to downplay what we saw as I described to Steve the two cuts on his head.

"It's almost nothing. I doubt it will even leave a scar. We just can't let anyone know about it."

Before we left, we used the last of the jug of water to wash the dried blood out of Steve's hair. It stung, and he shrieked a little, but I talked to him in the soothing tone of a good TV nurse. I needed him to cooperate so no one got in trouble. Montie was a little more direct.

"Quit whimpering! You're lucky to be alive. That arrow could have gone right through your brain!"

He was right, but we didn't necessarily need to hear it.

By the time we all got up to leave, you could hardly tell that anything had happened. Steve would surely be a little careful when combing his hair for a couple of weeks. But if we all played it cool, no one would ever know. And no one did. In a week or so, it was lost in farm-kid history. There were new and just-as-stupid exploits to take its place.

We never played the "Dodge the Red Arrow" game again. Not because we learned from our mistakes but because I eventually lost my only arrow. The bow even gave it up one day when Montie and I were shooting homemade arrows. We had made some arrows out of slender oleander branches. The arrows were way too long, but we decided to try it anyway. I pulled the bow back as far as I could pull and launched the crude arrow into the air. It was fun to watch the wobbly thing fly. So, we tried an even longer arrow, but my short arms couldn't pull it back far enough. To remedy the problem, we took the bow and clamped it in a pipe vise that was bolted to a wooden bench outside of our shop. I nocked the seven-foot-long arrow, stepped back, and pulled the string back with both hands. Just before I let it go, the fiberglass bow snapped, with a piece hitting me in the forehead, barely missing my eye.

And just like that, we got to replay the bloody mess of "fix it quick, before a parent finds out." A million cuts, bruises, falls, stunts, dares, and general stupidity flew under our parents' radars. But occasionally, some appalling stunt would get to the surface and land in their laps. It was always the same.

"What the hell's wrong with you, Rawge? Don't you have a lick of common sense?"

Looking back, I should have just said, "No, I'm a boy, and I'm not thirty years old yet!"

And just for the record, DO NOT TRY THIS AT HOME!!

12

Butterflies & Busted Stitches

Anything can be deadly, even a butterfly.

I was a sickly kid. I was born with some issues — parts wrapped around other parts and parts that didn't quite work right. I spent a lot of time in a hospital when my poor parents could afford it. Or, I spent a lot of time at home, likely needing to be in a hospital when they couldn't afford it.

When I was about two years old, I spent some time with lung issues, trying to shake a lingering bout of pneumonia. I was allergic to Penicillin, the most powerful antibiotic available. Replacements weren't as good. But after a few months of worrying my poor momma to death, I got over it.

Next, I had recurring tonsillitis. During one bout, when my throat became so swollen that I couldn't breathe, out came the tonsils. I was assured that they were accessories and I'd be just fine without them. After a few days of eating ice cream, I was fine.

For the next ten years, little by little, I got healthier. I'd have a problem occasionally, but they got fewer and farther apart. By the time I was ten, I was as healthy as any other farm kid who only washed his hands at dinner, and even then, only when Momma told me to.

But on one hot summer night, something happened. I woke from a deep sleep with sharp pains in my stomach. Soon, the pain moved to my side. I held my hand against it, hoping it would just go away. I lay in bed, concentrating on the hum of the swamp-cooler just down the hall. Surely the pain will go away. I just needed to wait.

But it didn't go away. The pain got worse. It reached a point where I was afraid. I was sure that I was dying. I stepped out of bed and doubled over from the pain. I told myself that I just needed to get down the hall to tell Mom. But I couldn't stand back up. All I could do, there on my knees, was to cry out for her.

The swamp-cooler was loud, but Momma heard me on my first scream. Within seconds, I could feel her reassuring bare feet pounding up the hall. In another second, she was on her own knees in front of me, asking me where it hurt.

My face and tears gave away the severity of the pain. Dad carried me gently outside to the car as my mom swapped a housecoat for pants and a blouse. I lay in a fetal position on the front seat while Mom drove the Buick, as fast as the roads would allow, to the hospital in Lemoore. They'd seen me before. I had a file. I had x-rays. They knew me.

I had appendicitis and a rupture. There were only two doctors in Lemoore, Dr. Guernsey, the oldest, and the younger Dr. Hall, his son-in-law. A ruptured appendix is life-threatening, even more so for a sickly kid who can't handle the best antibiotics. In an hour, Dr. Guernsey was scrubbed up and ready to remove the offending organ. Again, I was assured that it was just something extra that God had put into us and that I'd be fine without it. I had an emergency surgery, was started on antibiotics, and the healing began.

I spent a week in the hospital. I was happy to be back in the Buick, with Mom driving much slower, for the trip home. I had a gruesome set of stitches in the lower right side, below my belly. It literally made me feel sick to look at them. But I'd get them removed in just a few days.

When we got home, Mom and Dad had set me up to spend the next few days in their bed. It was the nicest room in the house. It had its own bathroom and big casement windows on each side. Butterfly bushes and jasmine vines were blooming just outside the window. With some of the windows on each side open, a scented breeze blew through the bedroom. There were enough pillows that I could prop myself up to read, and I had plenty of books.

It hurt to walk, but I managed to slowly get from the car to the bedroom. I was not to get out of bed for a few days. If I had to use the bathroom, Mom would help me there and back. She gave me only one command, "Stay in bed and get better."

By the second morning, I was already feeling better. Mom came in and brought me breakfast. She drew the curtains back and opened a window on each side of the room. Two of the windows were missing their screens, so they were only there to let sunlight in.

As I lay in bed, I could see the long purple bunches of flowers on the shrubs just outside the window. I could hear mockingbirds and mourning doves. I could feel a cool morning breeze blowing across my face. This was a place to recover and get well.

Everything was perfect. Except, I wasn't a kid who was much interested in staying in bed. As I lay in the comfortable bed, propped up on pillows, I saw something out of the window. Something important to me. Just outside, flittering on the purple lilac flower, was a beautiful tiger swallowtail.

In my bedroom down the hall, I had a butterfly net and an insect collection that I had started at the end of the previous summer. Pinned to a little block of Styrofoam, I had various butterflies, dragonflies, and beetles. I even had some wasps and a honeybee. What I didn't have was a big, yellow tiger swallowtail butterfly.

Within a second, I was sitting on the edge of the bed. I was sure that I could quietly make the few steps to my room, grab the net, and return to the open window. If I opened the window without a screen, I convinced myself that it would be easy to reach the net out a few feet and grab the yellow treasure.

The hall was only about twenty feet long, but every step was painful. I would take about five steps and then stop for long breaths. Five more steps. Five more steps. I had the net in my hand. Five more steps. Five more steps. Then I was sitting on the edge of the bed. I looked down at my bandage. I hurt, but everything was fine.

I looked towards the window., I couldn't see the butterfly but I wasn't quite ready to stand up again. I half-hoped that it was gone and wouldn't come back until I was well. I looked back down at my bandage and then back up towards the window. There it was, its yellow wings in beautiful contrast to the purple flowers.

I quickly stood up and shuffled to the closed window. I cranked the handle until it was wide open. I stretched my arm and net through the window and reached for the unsuspecting butterfly. But it was just out of reach. I needed six more inches. Through the pain, I leaned in closer and stood high up on the tippy-toes of one foot, the other foot with a bent knee to add that very last bit of length to my body. I reached. Then I reached a little more. I stretched every last muscle in my body.

And then my toes slipped. I heard a ripping sound that human bodies are not supposed to make, and then I felt the searing pain.

I got myself back to the bed and laid back. I couldn't bear to look. I hoped, at first, that maybe it was just the bandage that had torn away from my skin. After a minute or so, I looked down towards my bandage. It seemed in place. I slowly peeled back a corner until I could see my wound. I saw stuff that you're not supposed to see. It was bad!

As always, my first instinct was *DON'T TELL MOM*. Usually, it was in an attempt to save me from trouble or punishment, but occasionally, it was to shield her from grief or worry. A kid with ripped stitches and a butterfly net in his hand hit squarely in both categories.

This was serious. I couldn't not tell her. The pain became so severe that it made it easy for me to yell, "Mom!"

Again, she was there before I finished the scream.

"Roger Dale Jones! What have you done?"

"Oh, Momma, I was just trying to capture a butterfly through the window. It was a tiger swallowtail, and I don't ha...."

I didn't even get the words out, and we were back in the Buick, driving back to the hospital at break-neck speeds.

As Momma carried me in, she only told them that I had tripped and fallen. She didn't mention butterflies. She left the story wide open to a bathroom slip on a slippery floor. Doctor Guernsey stitched me back up. That second set of stitches would leave me with a big scar.

Within a day, I ended up with an infection and spent another week in the hospital. My fever was so high that the nurses would wipe my whole body down with alcohol. And several of the fevered days, I can't even remember.

I survived. Mom and the Buick, on the other hand, were both a little worse for wear. But that hospital stay started me down another stretch of ill health. By the time I celebrated my twenty-first birthday, I had suffered a bout with shingles. I got to hear a doctor tell me how rare it was for the disease to break out in someone so young! Next, I contracted a virus that caused me another hospitalization, dropped my weight by seventy-five pounds, and left me looking like a human skeleton! Later, I had an eye infection that ended with me wearing patches on both eyes for a week! To top it all off, I developed a big tumor under my armpit in one of my lymph nodes. It was removed and sent to a lab for analysis. For two weeks, I prayed and waited for the results. Thank God it was benign!

And there was more.

But then, at twenty-five years old, my health changed. I moved from the valley to northern California to attend college in Davis. College life was difficult, and my stress level was off the charts on a good day. But for the next thirty years, I hardly had as much as a cold. I didn't see the inside of a hospital and only saw a doctor for a check-up when my health insurance insisted.

The Pandemic changed all of that. On April 4, 2020, when we were all wearing bandannas, spraying Lysol, and still just trying to process the Coronavirus, I was in the emergency room. I lived in the hospital for the next month, on a ventilator and then on oxygen. I came home a different man and faced a new life in a full-blown pandemic.

But I lived. I was 60 years old then.

My mom died younger. She was only 59. I know that she was supposed to live to be one hundred. I'm sure that there was truth in her statement every time she looked at one of us and said, "You just took a year off my life! Don't ever do that again!"

I believe it. I'm sure of it.

Any grown man had better be able to look at his life and learn from every mistake.

I can. I've learned.

I want to grow old with the woman I love. So, don't laugh when you hear me say, "Please don't tell Rhonda!"

I need her to live to a hundred!

13

Life is Too Short for Whining

I vividly remember a hot afternoon, standing before Judge Aubrey H. Seed. I was sixteen, and it was my third speeding/speed exhibition ticket. I knew he was about to take my new license away. That license was my freedom.

My mom was with me in court. Neither of us called it a witch hunt. No one said I was being singled out. There was no mention that the judge must be crooked. I didn't call the court clerk names or say she had a low IQ. Nope.

I also didn't blame anyone else. I didn't blame my dad for getting me a 1970 El Camino SS with a big block, 4:11 rear-end, and shift kit. I didn't blame anyone else or ask the judge what about others who had done worse.

The only thing I thought about was that if you commit the crime, then you do the time. The gavel came down.

I said, "Yes, your honor," and handed him my license. I spent the next few weeks humbly riding the bus to school again.

A couple of years earlier, when I ran for a student council position and lost, I never said it was rigged. I never once said that I'm Rawge, so there's no way I lost. I can promise you that I did not call the office secretary who counted the votes and tell her that I just needed her to find forty-seven more votes, one more than the winner had.

I can also assure you that I didn't spend the next year whining about it every single day and raging about it every night.

Nope. I broke the law. I paid the price.
I lost the election. I went on about life.
But I guess that's kid stuff.
Adults have the freedom to act differently.

14

Bull Riders & Momma's Boys

There are hundreds of sports in this world. As kids, we're encouraged to explore them and get involved with something that interests us. On the surface, the door seems wide open. But in reality, a kid will more likely need to look around, close to home, to see what's available.

I wanted to learn how to sail. I had seen sailing ships on TV. I loved the big pirate ships, but the smaller ones that required just a person or two drew most of my attention. I was so interested that I built a little wooden sailboat, complete with two masts and cloth sails stretched across. My dad would drive me over to the yard at the cotton gin, where a big shallow pond would accumulate when it rained. I'd work on my ship, and then we'd go test it out.

The first launch just saw the boat tip over. Dad explained to me about ballast. You need weight at the bottom of the boat to counteract the capsizing forces of the wind on the sails. The lower it is in the ship, the less weight is needed. So I headed back to the drawing board.

After a few trips back and forth over the coming days, I had a little boat that would float with sails that caught the wind. On one particular day, there was the perfect amount of tiny wind. Dad asked me if my boat was ready for another launch. We drove the mile or so to the cotton gin. Pops watched while I sat the boat at the upwind edge of the pond. I adjusted the sails and let it go. I cheered as it sped across the water in perfect sailboat fashion. Pops yelled out, "It looks like you've got it!" I was proud.

I retrieved it from the other side of the pond and ran back to do it again. I sailed the pond a dozen times or more. I made some minor adjustments each round, and each time, it sailed straighter and faster than before. I had done it. I had built a sailboat.

But that's as far as my sailing career reached. I was a kid in the middle of the San Joaquin Valley. We were a hundred miles from a lake and even farther from the ocean. Sailing wasn't an option for me.

Sailing wasn't an option. Neither was fencing. I loved swords, but the closest I got to fencing was if I was stretching barbed wire and building it! Any sport that involved swimming was out. We swam in dirty irrigation ditches. Tennis and golf were out, and Momma said my face was way too pretty for boxing. To make things worse, I wasn't overly interested in anything that involved throwing, catching, or dribbling a ball. I was running out of options.

So, I started looking around closer to home. I took stock of what we had. The list was short. We had a couple of horses, one cow, a couple of goats, and a sheep. It didn't take long until I committed—I'd become a rodeo star!

The rodeo has a number of different events. In some of them, you use a specially trained horse and a rope to capture animals. In other events, you just ride animals that do not want you to ride them. There was bareback bronc riding where the cowboy rides a saddleless wild bucking horse. The rider uses only one hand to grip a little leather handle that is strapped on the horse's withers. Saddle-bronc riding does about the same thing, except the rider sits in a saddle, holding a rope tied to the horse's head. Bull riding was similar to the bucking horse events, except in the horse events, when you get bucked off, the horses don't then try to kill you. In bull riding, even if you manage to stay on for the eight-second ride, you've still got to contend with a ton of angry, snorting beef that wants to stick a horn or hoof through you before you can run to the safety of the fence.

I didn't have any specially trained horses, so those events would have to wait. I also didn't have any wild bucking horses, so those events would also have to wait. I didn't have any bulls, but I had a half-grown calf and a sheep, so I figured I'd start there and work my way up.

In planning for my future, at dinner time, I put an order in with Dad that

I needed a pony. At the same time, I made sure he didn't have any strong issues with me trying to ride the sheep or the calf. He told me simply, sure, just don't get hurt. As with most things, he was more concerned with the cost of a doctor's bill than he was with my eight-year-old bones.

The next day, my brother Steve agreed to help me corner the sheep long enough for me to jump onto its back. When I did, it ran across the pasture as fast as it could run. With nothing but wool to hold onto, I didn't last long and tumbled onto the hard pasture ground. Steve clapped and laughed.

We hemmed the sheep into a corner and tried it again. I lasted a little longer. We managed to get about six rides in before the sheep became uncatchable. It had figured out what was going on. We'd have to try the calf.

The calf weighed about seven hundred pounds and was tame since it had been raised with a bottle. We could walk right up to it. We led it over to a wooden gate and got it to stand next to one of the posts. We tied a rope around it so I had something to hold onto. I put my hand into it and jumped on. It startled the calf. The glorified pet ran a little way and actually bucked a time or two. But then it just stopped.

Steve walked over and slapped it on the haunch. It ran a few steps again and bucked another time or two. But then it was over. It's fight was done. At that point, I could have put a bridle on it and ridden it into town.

For the next month or so, I rode anything I could climb onto. A couple of miles from our house was an area of shoddy pens and little paddocks. People from our farm and others kept every animal imaginable there. I rode them all. I rode a half-dozen different goats and even jumped onto the back of a three-hundred-pound pig, just for fun. I wasn't getting any better at riding, but at that point, it was more about confidence, and I wasn't afraid to hop on anything.

A few months later, there was a junior rodeo in nearby Coalinga. Mom helped me send in the entry for the Wild Pony Riding event. I was excited and sure that I'd win. Mom sewed me a yellow long-sleeved cowboy shirt with fancy black piping at the yokes. I had boots and a couple of worn-out cowboy hats. I was ready.

On the day of the event, Mom got me signed in, and they gave me a big card with a number on it and safety pins to stick it on my back. Mom suggested that we wait until closer to my event to pin it on. I insisted that I wanted it on right then. I wanted to walk around with it so everyone knew I was in the rodeo, not simply a spectator.

When it came time for the Wild Pony Riding, there were about twenty kids entered. I watched as kid after kid fell off the little jumping ponies. When it was my turn, I walked up to chute number six. I stood on the platform above the chute and looked down at the brown pony. It stood calmly like it was trained to stand there.

The old cowboy who was working the event asked me if I was ready.

"Yep," I nodded.

"Are you nervous?"

"Nope!"

"Okay, climb on," he said as he pointed to the pony's back.

I sat down and slid my hand into the rigging. I took a deep breath and nodded for them to open the chute gate.

In a flash, the gate flew open. The little pony swung out and headed for the opposite side of the arena, straight towards the crowd. It didn't buck much but mostly just ran. It was an easy ride. I think even the fat farm pig was more animated. But when the loud buzzer went off at eight seconds, I pulled my hand out, swung my leg over, and hopped off.

The dismount was near perfect as I landed on my feet just in front of the bleachers. The crowd clapped, and a few of them hooted.

I was hooked! I ended up winning second place and got a nice big red ribbon to hang on my bedroom wall.

A few months later, my dad showed up one evening with a pony, a bridle, and a little saddle. Ponies are notorious for being mean. They bite and kick and are nearly useless. My pony, Foxy, was none of that. This little palomino-colored horse was sweet and loved to be ridden. When I walked into the pasture, it would trot right over to me, hoping to get fed a sugar cube or two. I could climb onto its back with neither a saddle nor a bridle, and it would just stand patiently and let me pat it on its neck. If I ran at it from the rear, it would turn as if it were ready to kick me. But it wasn't. It was setting up for me to do a flying mount, where I slapped both hands above its tail and flew onto its back.

Foxy was the perfect little horse. We went everywhere. We rode to other farms to visit my friends. We walked the dirt roads on full moon nights. She was careful and sure-footed. When we had visitors, I could show off by squeezing my legs while slightly pulling back on the reins. With that cue, Foxy would rear up and paw the air with her front legs.

But ponies are the biggest injustice in the entire universe. No matter how much you love, care for, and get attached to them, it's just a short matter of time until you outgrow them. They're done growing. But an eight-year-old kid isn't.

Within a couple of years, I was too big to ride Foxy. Dad managed to trade her to a guy for an actual horse. I wanted a horse, but I wanted to keep my friend as well. But Dad said that just wasn't right, she's such a good pony that some other young kid should get to have the same experience as I did. I knew he was right, but that didn't stop the tears when she disappeared up the road in a horse trailer.

Through the years, I had other horses and went on to compete in most every rodeo event—team roping, calf roping, bull-dogging, and others. I was terrible at all of them. I would compete in a couple dozen rodeos each year. But it was futile. It didn't matter how much I practiced, and I practiced a lot. I never got any better. I've thrown a million loops at a hay bale with horns attached, but it didn't matter. I never got better. I spent a thousand Wednesday evenings at The Caballo Club rodeo grounds in Coalinga. I'd take my horse and practice team roping for hours. It didn't matter. I never got better.

By my high school years, I was done. I'd likely never win anything, and it wasn't much fun. The comradery was wonderful. I enjoyed every minute of hanging out with my cowboy friends, but I lost all interest in the competitive part. As a teenager I lost all interest in all of it, except one event—bull riding!

To read a line like that, you would quickly reason that I was very likely a star. I wasn't. I was as bad at bull riding as I was at every other event. But in bull riding, it didn't matter as much about how good you were at it. It only mattered that you did it.

During the roping events, the bleachers were always near empty. The only people who cared much to watch it were your friends or relatives. As soon as you made your run, they returned to talking and whatever they were doing a minute before. But when the bull riding event rolled around, every person stopped to watch. To a high school boy, every person meant every high school girl!

Bull riders had clout, and they had clout with girls. If you had acne and bad hair, you had less acne and better hair if you mentioned that you were a bull rider. If you stuttered and couldn't look a girl in the eyes, your confidence was suddenly bolstered just at the mention that you were a bull rider. Those two words were the icebreaker and opening line in any awkward conversation with a girl.

"What event are you doing?"

That was your cue to clench your jaw, stare into the distance, and say, "I'm a bull rider."

But even then, I knew that bull riders were an odd bunch. Most every one of them had some manner of weird ritual before they rode. I'd seen everything from splashing a handful of nasty arena dirt onto their face to jumping down and hammering out exactly twenty-three push-ups before they walked up to the chute. One odd cowboy would have a friend slap him in the face thirteen times as quickly as possible.

I didn't have any pre-ride rituals. I considered all of them dumb and nobody was going to slap me in the face. But I did have one post-ride ritual that I adhered to without fail. The very moment my ride was over, I walked straight to a payphone and called my mom. If I had to beg, borrow, or steal a dime and a quarter, I wasn't missing that call.

"Mom, I'm done."

She never asked how I did or how I scored. She asked only three questions.

"Are you okay? Are you hurt? Did you break anything?"

"Nope, Momma, I'm fine."

"Okay, I love you. I'll see you when you get home."

"I love you, too, Momma. I'll see you soon."

So, I was a bull rider.

Well, first and foremost, I was a momma's boy.

Years later, when my momma died, she left a box under her bed with my name on it.

Inside, she'd kept my red Wild Pony Riding ribbon. She had kept almost every rodeo number and program that I had brought home. She had newspaper clippings from our little local paper that mentioned my name on the rare occasions when I won something. The box had a Polaroid picture of me holding the first trophy buckle that I had won.

I went through the box with teary eyes. I wondered how many hours she had spent sitting by the phone, waiting for her brave bull-rider son to call home and tell her I was okay.

For an hour, this brave bull rider sat and cried like a baby.

My bull-riding days are all long gone.

But I'll be a momma's boy until the day I die.

15

Idiots

When I was a teenager, I was out sitting on my tailgate, mad about something or how someone had treated me. My dad drove up and stepped out of his truck. Out of the blue, I told him, "I just don't understand idiots!"

He didn't hear exactly what I said. He responded, "Take one apart, look in, and see how it works."

I busted up laughing.

Pops just looked at me and asked, "What's so funny?"

I said, "Idiots. Take one apart?"

He then busted up laughing, too. "I thought you said SPIGOTS!"

A few days before, he had me rebuild two big leaky faucet valves on one of our wells, so it was an honest mistake. But he might have accidentally been onto something.

If we don't understand an idiot, take one apart and look inside—metaphorically speaking, of course!

I think that there's really no such thing as an idiot. But there are plenty of people who seem to make dumb decisions or have ridiculous behavior. I think it would do us well to have a "look inside" before we get overly judgy. Who knows what influences someone might have, or what has happened in their lives, or what they're going through now.

I think Pop's inadvertent admonishment to open one up and look inside was really just a different way of saying, "Walk a mile in their shoes," before you start calling someone names. It's pretty good advice.

Just for the record, I say that there's really no such thing as an idiot. But I must admit, Washington, D. C., sure makes me wonder. 🐾

16

It's Clearing Up

Everyone on this planet has a particular outlook on life. We see the bright side or the dark side. Some see the glass as half-empty, while others see it as half-full. Some see the glass and don't care. We just know that whatever it is, it's refillable.

Some of the ways that we view life and our circumstances are hereditary. We all know some people who are just prone to worry. They just can't help it. It's in their genes. I've been there.

Some of the ways that we view life are situational. Whether we are in good times or hard times can shape our view. I know that we've looked at friends or family and thought, "I remember when they used to be so happy and optimistic. I wonder what happened?" Sometimes, it's the opposite, and we look at others and think to ourselves, "Wow! They sure have a new outlook on life!"

But sometimes, our view of life is learned. Regardless of what's going on around us, we've been encouraged, or even demanded, to always see the bright side!

Last year, Rhonda and I were on a cruise along the Mexican Riviera and through the Panama Canal. One morning, I was in the ship's elevator and shared a ride with a gentleman. He was about five feet tall, bald-headed, and wearing a big smile. I said good morning and asked him, "How are you doing today?"

He looked at me with a smile and said, "If I was any better, vitamins would be taking me!!!"

I know his outlook on life!

I've got an old friend who can't help but see the bright side of life. I've never seen him without a smile. I've jokingly said that if for some weird reason, he was sent to jail, he'd just smile and say, "Well, I've always loved wearing stripes!"

I know his outlook on life!

When I was a kid on the farm, we all worked. Often, I'd be driving a tractor, plowing, discing, or planting a crop. Like any other kid who felt that they shouldn't have to work, I always hated it. We worked a lot. Thanks to my dad's ridiculous superstitious nature, we'd get random days off, like every Friday the thirteenth or when he saw a black cat cross the road. But other than that, if there was work to be done, then we were out doing it, rain or shine.

To a farmer, rain is both a blessing and a curse. It all depends on when you get it and how much you get. Rain at the wrong time could mean fields too muddy to work or seeds that rot before they sprout. If you get it too late, fields dry up, and you can watch the precious soil blow away in the wind.

To us kids, rain was always a blessing. We didn't pray for a gentle rain to pass by and water our crops or settle the dust. We prayed for pounding rain that meant it was too wet to work. We wanted muddy fields and muddy roads. We wanted every tractor parked at the shop and a dirt road so muddy that a tractor couldn't even get us to our bus stop.

Many times, I remember sitting in a tractor seat, watching the clouds on the horizon. I'd watch as they got closer and closer and darker and darker. Soon, I could see the big raindrops hitting the dust on the tractor's fenders. With crossed fingers, I'd look across the fields and hope for more.

As the rain slowly wet the tractor, and then the field, and then me, I'd hope to see my dad coming up the road, flashing the lights on his four-wheel drive pickup. Flashing headlights was our signal to shut things down.

But my dad saw rain differently. He needed the work to be done. He needed fields plowed. He needed everything that led to a successful crop. Dad needed bales of cotton at the end of the year or tons of barley seed. My dad had bills to pay, and he fought against the rain.

Those wet farm days started a saying in our family and around our farm. So many times, I'd park at the end of the field, and Dad would hop out of his truck. He'd bend his head down, away from the wet wind, hustle over to my tractor, and step up towards the driver's seat.

"It's pouring down, Dad! Let's park it and go home!" I'd yell to him against the sound of the wind and the rain.

But my pops would just turn his face up towards the black sky, with the wind drenching his face, and then turn back to me with his familiar response, "Naw, it's clearing up!"

Maybe he saw a hint of blue somewhere on the horizon. Maybe he somehow saw the thinnest ray of sunshine in the dark distance. But whatever he saw or didn't see, that phrase became part of the ranch lexicon. My dad said it hundreds of times. It was an optimistic phrase.

I knew his outlook on life.

In 2020, I had spent a month in the hospital, and a few of those days, I'd knocked at death's door. Even after I was sent home with failing lungs, I was sure that I'd die. But at least I'd die at home.

On one particularly dark night, I couldn't breathe. My chest was heavy and full, and no amount of coughing could relieve it. The oxygen I received through my nose was set to maximum, and still, I was suffocating. I sat in my chair, trying to cough, as each one became more difficult. It takes a lot of muscle to cough, and I didn't have much left. I was afraid to fully tell Rhonda my fears. It was still during the peak of COVID-19, and a trip in an ambulance would mean that she and I would be separated again. I had just spent a month without her, and I would rather die than be separated again.

Rhonda sat beside me with her hand on my shoulder. She gently told me everything would be alright—she had said it many times. She calmly told me that it was just another rough night but that I'd get through it, too. She encouraged me, "When you can, just try again."

I sat up as straight as I could, and with as deep a breath as I could muster, I coughed again. It forced the air completely through to clear my lungs. Finally,

I felt relief.

And in a moment, my mind said, "It's clearing up!" I smiled. I smiled for that moment and for the beautiful memories of my dad.

It did clear up. And the next bad night cleared up as well. The next bad month cleared up, and the next year cleared up.

So, I live with that simple phrase lingering in my mind. It pops up when things are at their worst or at their darkest. We say it around our house, and our grandkids say it.

"It's clearing up!"

And now you know my outlook on life.

17

Bad Haiku

I still have an old notebook that I used in junior high school. My mom saved it and held it in a box until she died. It has about fallen apart, but I keep it to show me how far I've come.

It's full of ramblings by a kid who someday wants to be an artist, an author, or something else besides a farmer.

The blue cover and dog-eared pages are full of bad drawings and sketches, badly written scribblings of stories that I wanted to *someday* write, and plenty of bad poetry.

It has one especially bad Haiku.

My wheel is squeaky
The kids can hear me coming
Yes WD-40

Fifty years later, I have two published books full of ramblings by a grown-up kid who still wants to be an artist, an author, or anything else besides a farmer!

18

Music is Magic

I was born and raised around music. My Papa Kinley was a fiddler, and he fiddled every day of his life. His brothers and sisters, my great aunts and uncles, played instruments as well, and several of them sang. My dad loved music and would drag my brother and me to bluegrass festivals around California.

Music was everywhere I went as a kid. It came from Papa and Grandma's front yard or porch, a record player in our house, or a radio in our car or truck. I never thought much about it back then, but it was everywhere.

My wife, Rhonda, and I have played music together for 20 years. We've spent a thousand or more Sundays playing, singing, and encouraging others to lift their voices in church. We've played concerts. We've played at open mic nights. We've played in parks and parking lots. Music remains an essential part of our lives.

I know we both got music burned into our souls at a young age. Me on the farm, and Rhonda from her dad. Music is something that sticks. It's powerful. It's beautiful. And whether you're making the music or just tapping your foot along to it, it's evocative.

A friend of mine is a wonderful piano player. She has music in her soul. She's retired, travels around to convalescent centers, and plays piano for the older folks. She has told me stories about how the music lifts everyone's spirits. People get up from their chairs and wheelchairs and clap and dance.

Music is in their souls, too. Music moves them from today into other times in their lives. A morning in church seventy years ago. A high school dance sixty years ago. A concert in a park with their love, fifty years ago. Music is magic, and it can be like a time machine.

Several years ago, Rhonda was the music leader at a church just down the road from our house. She had a great team of talented musicians. We practiced for a couple of hours each Wednesday evening. I stood in the back of the church platform with my acoustic guitar. On my left was an electric guitar player, and on my right was Crissy, our violin player. Not many church music groups have the luxury of a violin, and Crissy was excellent.

Late on one Wednesday afternoon, I headed for our evening practice. I sometimes came straight from a long workday, tired and not really in the mood. I pulled into the parking lot a little early and looked around at the cars to see who was already there. Other than Rhonda, Crissy's was the only other car in the empty lot. She often got there early and warmed up with beautiful violin tunes on the stage.

The church doors open into a big foyer, and then the foyer doors open into the sanctuary. With both sets of doors closed, you cannot hear anything in the parking lot. But during practice, we usually left the foyer doors open. As I was getting my guitar case out of the back seat of my truck, someone opened the church door to walk in. The door opened wide and then very slowly began to close. In those few seconds, while the door was gently closing, I could hear Crissy's violin. It was distant, but I could hear the high strings and the haunting drone of the open, low strings as she drew her bow. It was magic.

And in that moment, it captured my spirit. I felt what the old folks felt when they heard a sound or song from their childhood. I was instantly moved to another time and place.

When I was a small child, living on our big farm, everyone worked. When your hand could wrap completely around a hoe or shovel handle, you were expected to work, too. This was especially true in the summer when our one-thousand acres of cotton were getting tall, and the weeds were getting taller. Weeds were a farmer's enemy. Wherever there was a weed, there wasn't a cotton plant and a cotton plant was money. A weed stole precious water from the ground and nutrients from the soil. Weeds came in a hundred different sizes and colors. A single weed was a problem. A thousand weeds were a big problem. No matter their color, ten thousand weeds were the difference in finishing the year in the red or finishing in the black.

Summer mornings started at five o'clock a.m. Even as the sun came up, the farm was a buzz of activity. As many as a hundred people, mostly ladies, began to assemble at the end of a cotton field. This was the hoe crew. The ladies wore big hats to keep the sun off their faces and billowy, long-sleeved shirts to keep the sun off their arms. They toted jugs of water in colorful coolers or plain white milk jugs and carried lunch in paper grocery bags.

Just as the sun came up, each person grabbed a hoe from a big pile on the side of the dirt road and lined up on a cotton row. My Papa Kinley was the hoe boss. He got each person on the correct row and made sure that nothing got skipped. He followed behind the younger people now and then to make sure they were doing a good job and not missing anything. He kept the hundred or so hoes as sharp as razors.

When all the grown ladies went to the fields each morning, they left behind their children. Some were watched by older brothers and sisters, an aunt or uncle who was sick or hurt and couldn't work, or most anyone they could find to babysit for eight or ten hours. When my mom left, I stayed with Grandma Elsie.

Even when Grandma had a dozen kids to watch, every day was fun. We'd play in the yard while she kept a watchful eye from a chair on her porch. Through the chaotic scene of the front yard daycare, Grandma still managed to find some moments to talk to me. They were close talks. Her words were heartwarming and lasting. I was six years old, but I remember them.

Farming is a constant job of trying to stay one step ahead of calamity. More often than not, it's one step behind. Without fail, at some point in the summer, the hoe crew would get behind. My dad would put out the word that he needed more people. He'd get teenagers showing up and maybe even a wino or two from town who wanted to make a little money. But at some point, Grandma Elsie would head for the field. Maybe my dad needed the labor, or maybe Grandma just needed the money, but either way, the carefree daycare was closed.

This was a horrible time for me. There were days when we didn't have anyone else to watch us kids. My sisters were at the field, and my mom was at the field. On these dark days, six-year-old Rawge got dragged to the fields. I didn't work. But it was worse. I just followed along behind my mom—step after step, row after row. A day was an eternity.

The hoe crew worked like a giant living machine. Each person walked down a furrow, weeding each row beside them. They walked slowly, moving their heads from side to side to see the small weeds hidden below the growing cotton. One hundred workers equaled two hundred rows. Every field was exactly one half-mile long. When the crew reached the end of the field, the person on the outside stepped over two furrows and held up their arm. The rest of the crew filled in, taking every other furrow until everyone was standing in a row. Then, they started through the field again. It was up and back all day.

Sometimes, there were not many weeds, and a worker could walk at a near-normal pace. But other times, the weeds were thick, causing the pace to slow to a crawl. If someone had an especially weedy row and fell behind, one of the older ladies would jump back to help them through a weedy patch. It was hot and dusty, but the ladies chatted with each other throughout the day. Each worker was only three feet from the person on their right or left, so there was a lot of talking going on. If you had a sensitive subject, like gossip, and needed some privacy, you just slowed down and slipped back a little, away from prying ears. It took about forty-five minutes or more to make the one-mile round trip.

I was a little scrawny for my age and stood just over three feet tall. In late summer, the cotton was taller than me. I walked behind my momma like I was in a jungle. I couldn't see over the cotton or to the end of the field. I just watched the backs of my momma's feet and followed along. For the folks standing above the cotton, it was brutally hot. But below, where I walked, it was brutally hot and brutally humid. Before long, I'd be drenched in sweat.

When the crews all started into the field, my Papa stayed behind. He sat on a chair beside the pile of hoes and grabbed a file with a homemade wooden handle. He picked up each hoe, ran his thumb across the blade, and then used the file to sharpen any edge that wasn't perfect. One by one, he sat them back down with a crisp, shiny new edge. When the hoes were done, he made notes in a notebook, with the date, each person's name, and the hours they worked. Next, he'd pull his truck forward and move the beat-up portable bathroom along to keep up with the moving crew.

Papa stayed busy, but when the hoe sharpening, bathroom moving, and note-taking were done, he would have a few idle minutes on his hands. He would look out toward the crew, move his chair into the shade of a tarp he'd prop up around his truck bed, and sit down. Then he'd open up his fiddle case and start fiddling. He'd fiddle *"The Eighth of January."* Then he'd fiddle *"Old Joe Clark."* He could fiddle *"Redwing"* and fall right into *"Sally Goodin'."* He was a master.

As I plodded along behind my momma, I listened. I didn't listen to the chatter of gossip from a bunch of old ladies. I listened to the air. I got down low to the ground and listened. I stood on my tip-toes and cocked my ear toward the road. I listened like a man who had a hundred-dollar seat at the opera, waiting for that first note in the darkened theater. I listened for Papa's fiddle.

When it seemed close, I'd take a few steps and listen. Then I'd take a few more. Then a few more. Then...there it was! It was distant, but I could hear the high strings and the drone of the open low strings as Papa drew his bow. It was magic. I knew we were getting close to the end of the field!

The end of the field signaled relief. Everyone took a short rest and sat down. The end of the field meant shade and a big drink of water. Somewhere in the mass of old ladies, one of them would always pull a piece of cake out of a bag and hand it to the pitiful, sweaty, brown-haired boy. Someone else would offer a piece of candy in the direction of my brown eyes. Papa would continue to fiddle for the crowd. Sometimes, I'd clog and dance with the cake in one hand and the other, wiping sweat from my face. The end of the row was ten minutes of heaven, and Papa's fiddle announced it better than Gabriel's horn.

"Rawge!...Rawge!... you coming in?"

The voice seemed to come out of nowhere. Then, it seemed a little louder.

"Hey man, let's go in. Let's make some music."

I turned my head and slowly left the cotton fields of sixty years ago. I flew through time. It took me a few seconds to rejoin the moment. The voice was Terry, the other guitar player. He had pulled his truck in beside me and was ready to practice. I hadn't even noticed the parking lot filling up.

"You alright, man?"

"Yeah, I'm good."

"You were just standing there with a big smile on your face."

"Yep. I guess I was listening to Papa's fiddle."

Terry just shrugged and laughed.

Somewhere in there, I'd lost my bad mood. I walked inside with a happy feeling in my body. I was ready to make music. Music that would move people. Music that would lift people's spirits and lift their hands toward the heavens. Music that would stick in their soul for a hundred years.

I was ready to make music as powerful as memories.

19

Support the Arts

I belong to some internet discussion groups about various topics, ranging from music to literature. I'm not a great participant. I rarely have anything significant to add, so I mostly just lurk and read. Most of the posts and comments are pretty boring, but occasionally, someone poses a very thought-provoking question or topic.

One of the more interesting questions came from one of the music groups. Someone asked why our world no longer produces monumental, life-long works like Bach's Mass in B-minor or the Magnificat. Bach wrote over eleven hundred classic pieces that are performed and enjoyed today, almost three hundred years later.

When I read the question, I thought the same could be asked about any of the other arts. Why do we no longer produce pieces like Michelangelo's *Sistine Chapel Frescoes* or his statue of *David*? Or even great books like Tolstoy's *War and Peace* or Miguel de Cervantes's *Don Quixote*? These were great questions and made me stop to think.

After a few days of thinking about the question, I scrolled back to the forum to see what others had to say. There were not many comments, and most were the typical dull diatribe about the general collapse of society. These are always cop-outs that come from those people who feel that every generation is dumber, lazier, and less equipped for life than people of their generation. I agree that there's something to be said for those water-hose-drinking, truck-bed riding, lead paint licking, and no bike helmet-wearing survivors of the 1950s and 1960s, but the gentrification of society is not the answer to these questions.

As I read through a few pages of people's near-mindless thoughts, one netizen's response hit me differently. This deeper thinker had postulated that artists today have day jobs. No longer do we see benefactors finding struggling artists and setting them up with a house, food, servants, and most everything else they need in life so that they can dedicate themselves to art. Every day. All Day. For sixty years or more. Art all day and night. No day jobs.

I sat my phone down, leaned back in my easy chair, and thought about supporting the arts. I'll likely never find an artist and house them in a nice studio on the back of our property. I don't see myself running Rhonda's delicious meals to the back and setting them, along with some red wine, on a table outside the studio door. I doubt I'll pick up a basket of white cotton shirts or flowery dresses for their laundry. Nope, none of that will happen.

I thought more about it and ran through my mental list of the ways that Rhonda and I do support the arts. The things that rolled through my mind are small, but perhaps in a lifetime, they cumulatively make a difference in the world.

We never leave an art walk or craft fair empty-handed. Our house is full of clay bowls, small paintings, and jewelry. I'm sure there are artists out there who went home one day happy with their small sales.

We strive to attend local gigs when any of our musician friends are performing. We buy food and drinks from the venue and then leave a tip in the tip jars. We follow the artist's social media pages and comment on their works.

There's more. It's all small. But it's there.

As I sat in the dark, deep in thought, something came to mind that made me chuckle. With all of the art and artists in the world and all of the opportunities, there is one that I will absolutely one hundred percent never miss. Never ever.

When I was a kid, my dad and a handful of his farmer buddies took a trip to Mexico to fish for marlin. The trip was the first and only time my dad ever flew on a jet. The others on the trip were fairly well off. We weren't. I don't know how Pops managed it, but I bet he was the only person on the jet who was making payments on living room furniture.

The farmer group made it to Mazatlán, Mexico, had a blast, caught some marlin, and returned home. Dad brought a bag of Mexican coins for my collection. He told me all about the trip. He told me about hooking a marlin and how it jumped while he fought it for an hour. It was all so exotic and captivating to me. As a poor farm boy, the thrill of it all sunk in and changed me. I vowed that someday I would grow up and travel to Mexico.

I've since been in Mexico many times. For the past few years, Rhonda and I have stayed in Cabo San Lucas for a month at a time. I've caught marlin, dorado, tuna, and wahoo. Dad's short trip fifty years ago stuck with me and changed me. But there's more to it all. Something on his trip changed me and was buried even deeper into me.

On the second day of Pop's trip, they returned from a day of fishing. The boat captain had recommended a restaurant not far from their hotel. He told them that it was a fun place and that beer and tequila were cheap. I doubt that since the jet touched the tarmac in Mexico, Dad or his comrades had spent more than five minutes without a beer in their hands. They all liked to drink, but throwing cheap tequila in the mix was just asking for trouble.

As the sun set after the day of fishing, the group walked a few blocks and found an alley marked with a crudely painted sign. They walked halfway to the next block, and there it was, just as the boat captain had described. The little outdoor restaurant was more bar than restaurant, but they could smell the familiar aroma of authentic Mexican food drifting into the alley. The five farmers settled into a table and ordered some beers.

They drank their beer and ate their enchiladas and rice and beans. Soon, the waitress cleared their plates, and in regular order, she returned with more bottles of Pacifico and rounds of Mezcal. It's no surprise that as the full moon rose overhead, the group and most everyone in the bar were perfectly drunk.

As the tequila-dizzy farmers sat at the table, telling loud stories and laughing, they heard music coming up the alley. The sound of guitars and voices grew nearer, and with a burst of "Ay Yii Yi Yiiiiii," a group of mariachis stepped out of the darkness and into the bar. They stood at the steps and finished a rousing version of the old Mexican folk song, *"Alla En El Rancho Grande."* On the last note, they all gave big smiles and bowed. The fiesta-colored lights that hung across the front of the bar reflected on the beautiful musical instruments—the guitar, the big six-string bass called the guitarron, the trumpet, and the accordion.

A group of people in the back motioned for the band to come to their table. The group filed through the array of tables, circled the cheering gringos, and played them a song. When they finished to a round of applause, my dad waved them over to their table. Within a minute, the happy mariachis were standing in front of them.

In a loud drunken voice, one of Pop's friends yelled to the guitar player, the group's lead singer, "Play that Cook-a-racha song!"

His drunken voice came off more of a demand than it did a request. But the band smiled and started in. They knew the song. They had played it a million times for every drunk American who had visited Mexico. The breadth and depth of Mexican folk music is astounding. There are the traditional rancheria songs, as well as beautiful waltzes. There are lively polkas and somber ballads and danzóns. Mexican music is as varied as any music in the world. But Americans want to hear "La Cucaracha."

When the song finished, the farmers clapped and laughed. "Play it again. Come on, play it again!"

The mariachis looked at each other. What the heck? They started in again. *"La cucaracha, La cucaracha, ya no puede caminar!"*

This time, they played the song even louder and with more energy. Verse and then chorus, over and over. They sang about a cockroach that can't walk because it lost its two back legs. Maybe the crippled cockroach symbolized Victoriano Huerta Marquez, a Mexican general who became president. Perhaps it's about the Mexican bandit Pancho Villa's car. No one really knows. But all agree, it is a fun song.

As the mariachis sang the song, the leader watched the drunk farmers laughing and singing along to the familiar parts, so he started the whole song over and played it again. The song lasted 10 minutes. At the last word, the tired band ended with a loud, *"Cha Cha Cha!"*

The farmers gave a round of applause, and then bored with the music, they turned their attention back to each other and started right back to their jokes and loud laughter. The mariachis stood silently and patiently for a moment and then quietly shuffled out of the restaurant.

When the moon was directly overhead, the farmers had had enough fun for the night. They paid their bill and headed back towards their hotel rooms. They stumbled through the darkness in the alley, looking towards the dim light ahead on the street. About halfway there, at the darkest part of the walk, they heard voices and saw movement in the dark shadows.

As their eyes adjusted to the darkness, they watched each of the mariachi players step into the moonlight. Even in the dark alley, their clothes and sequins glistened. In a matter of seconds, the formerly talented musicians had taken on their alter-egos and turned into street-fighting tough guys. It only took a minute to leave the farmers on the ground, bloody and beaten.

To hear my dad say it, "They whooped our ass good!"

As the musicians walked away in the darkness, the leader of the group stopped to offer an admonition. Whatever the limits of his bilingual vocabulary, he offered two sentences in perfect English, "We don't get paid. We work for tips!"

As my dad told me that part of the story, he looked me in the eye and said, "We learned a lesson. ALWAYS TIP THE MARIACHIS!!!!"

I laughed. At ten years old, the thought of my dad and his buddies getting their asses whipped by a bunch of musicians was golden! And at that moment, I fell in love with mariachis!

As I mentioned earlier, Rhonda and I have visited Mexico many times. When we are in a restaurant, I'm the first to wave to the roving bands when they walk in. I will request an old song like *"Mi Rancho Grande"* or *"Quatro Milpas."* I've learned the songs and will even play the guitar with them if they let me.

We do not leave the hotel without a pocketful of five and ten-dollar bills.

I always, one hundred percent of the time, absolutely, every time, without

fail—tip the mariachis.
　　I don't want no trouble!
　　I support the arts!!!

20

From Grit to Shine

When I was a kid, one of my teachers gave me a polished rock that she had polished in a rock tumbler. It was small and fit perfectly into the palm of my little hand. She told me that some people call them worry stones. When you are worried, you can hold it while rubbing your fingers on its smoothness, and it is guaranteed to make you feel better.

I was a kid and had very few worries, but I still spent time rubbing the rock's beautiful, glossy, smooth sides. I told Mrs. Beilage that someday I'd get my own rock polisher. She advised me to pick up every interesting rock that I found and save it for the polisher. It would be forty years until I actually bought the little machine, but that didn't stop me from walking around with a pocket full of rocks from that day forward. Even today, not a week goes by that I don't get a stern look from Rhonda when we hear rocks clanking around in the clothes dryer.

Since those days, I've worn out a few tumblers, and I've surely polished a hundred pounds of rocks. I pick them up everywhere I go. I've made trips to the mountains and deserts and brought home buckets full in my truck. I've picked them up in other countries and brought them home in my luggage. I've picked them up on the beach and in my own backyard. If I'm walking, there's always a little piece of my brain looking for rocks.

The little stones pile up in buckets and coffee cans and wait for their chance to spend a month or more inside the noisy tumbler. The machine sits in my shop, spinning in circles, twenty-four hours a day, seven days a week.

As one of my monthly rituals, I sit down on a beautiful Saturday morning and unload the little batch of smooth stones. I pour them onto an outdoor table in our backyard sitting area and begin the process. One by one, I dry them off with a soft cloth, roll them around in my fingers, and give each stone a good inspection.

The whole process could take five minutes, but it takes me much longer. Every rock makes me think and reflect. Where did I find this little purple stone? Was it that day the three-wheeled taxi dropped us at a bench overlooking a beautiful little seaside town in the Canary Islands? Maybe it was that time my son Levi and I spent a week roaming around the deserts in Nevada. Or perhaps it was that time I was trout fishing in the Sierra mountains and rounded a turn of the creek to see a whole bank of shimmering rocks at my feet. Oh well, I can't remember. Move on to the next rock.

The other day, as I rifled through my buckets and cans to choose something perfect to refill the machine, I thought about the slow process in the tumbler. Sometimes, it takes months. I put in jagged rocks, broken, splintered, and covered in the crust of years. I seal them up and just let the water and grit slowly work on them, twenty-four hours a day. During the long process, the rocks tumble and clash with the others, slowly wearing off their jagged edges and taking on a new shape.

Next, I clean them up, add fresh water and new media, and start the process again. This time, the grit is finer. The rocks tumble, but it's not nearly as noisy. The ugly outer layer is gone, and the rock's true colors start to show.

When the process is done, and I get to spread them on the table, they are no longer just rocks. Now, they are beautiful stones and gems. They are almost unrecognizable from the ragged and rough rocks that I carried around in my pockets and dropped into the little machine.

As I pick up each beautiful stone from the pile on the table, roll it around in my hand, and hold it up to the light, I can't help but think about my own process.

Time and influence have worked on me, too. God started me tumbling, and then family and friends were added to the mix. As the sharp edges and grime were ground off, my life's experiences were poured in, followed by successes and failures and hopes and dreams.

I know I'm still tumbling and need more time, but love is in the mix now.

Yep, I'm still a rock. It's not a polished stone or certainly not a gem, but my true colors are really starting to show.

As I hold the jagged stones and think about the humor of my tumbling in life's polisher, I realize that there are some limits to the similarities. Rocks don't get to choose what goes into the tumble process—but I do! I choose what gets into the mix. I choose the people and circumstances that will grind off my jagged edges. I choose the influences that will bring out my shine. I choose the love that brings out that final gloss. I choose what I let in.

Now, I just need to remember. We're all still tumbling.

Every day and every night.

One of these days, I'm gonna shine!

21

Magnification

About thirty years ago, I was shopping with Rhonda in a department store in Sacramento. I get bored if I stay too long in one place, and we had spent way too much time looking at bed sheets. So, as a ruse to walk around, I pardoned myself to go locate the bathroom.

I found the bathrooms in short order and slowly meandered my way back to Rhonda. I passed by an aisle with several round mirrors. Not being one to pass up an opportunity to look at myself, I leaned forward and peeked into one that had a big "1X" marker on it. I moved my head from side to side to get a good look. "Yep," I thought, "that's a good-looking ol' boy," and leaned back to a standing position. I glanced around at the other mirrors sitting on the shelf. I noticed that as you moved down the shelf, the X-numbers got bigger. The last one on the shelf was marked "10X."

I walked a few steps and leaned into the biggest mirror.

Ahhhhhhhhh! What on God's green earth was that?!

I jumped back like a startled monkey who had just seen himself in a mirror for the first time.

It took a moment for me to collect myself, and then I looked around to make sure no one was watching. It seemed safe, so I slowly leaned forward to get another look. As I got close enough for the big mirror to get me into focus, I saw it again. Yep. I was disgusting! I was covered in black hair. I had giant black pores. My eyes were bloodshot. The thing looking back at me was more creature than human.

At the revelation, I hastily made my way back to Rhonda, trying my best to nonchalantly cover my face from strangers. I quickly found her and whispered, "Let's go!"

She responded with, "Why? What's wrong?"

"I'm hideous! That's what's wrong!"

I told her about the big mirror, and she laughed. We ended up buying the 10X so I could inspect myself in the privacy of my own home.

The mirror had taken something small and made it ten times bigger. It was gross, but I could flip it over and see myself at regular size.

The whole ordeal made me realize that there's not much in our lives that can handle the scrutiny of a magnifying glass. Even more importantly, not everything should. There's already plenty around us that ends up bigger than life-size, and it's not just mirrors that can blow things out of proportion. Social media can do it. The news can do it. Billboards can do it. TV ads can do it. Even friends and family can occasionally make our issues a little bigger. We need to be careful and ready to bring things back to 1X when necessary. I'm all for introspection and self-awareness, but sometimes we need to flip the mirror back to reality and just live the 1X life for a bit.

Just for the record, though. If I ever get shipwrecked on an island and I've been more than thirty days without my big mirror, tweezers, and scissors, I'll be unrecognizable as a human. Tell the rescuers not to shoot me. I'm a man. Really.

22

Burdens & Baggage

I recently had a long conversation with a friend. He's my age, but we only met later in life, yet we've gotten close. The conversation was one of those when you quickly sensed that the other person needed a confidant, someone to trust, someone who would listen to understand, not just listen to respond. On that day, I was that person.

As the conversation got deeper, he hinted at things he wasn't proud of in his life. He talked about his childhood and his brothers and sisters. He went on about his high school years and, later, his first marriage. I mixed a few words in here and there, but slowly he went on.

The friend talked about the jobs he held over the years before settling into his career. He talked about his wife and his family. He told me about his kids and their successes. He mixed in a few of their failures just so I knew they weren't all angels.

Throughout the whole conversation, he lightly highlighted decisions that he'd made. He seemed to linger on the areas with two paths and then tell me about the path that he had chosen. But more often, he talked about what may have been on the other path. He spoke of things he had done but also about things he hadn't done.

Sometimes he talked with a smile, and sometimes he didn't. Sometimes, he looked me in the eyes, and other times, he just looked out into the distance. He talked. I listened.

After an hour or so, he wrapped up by telling me that he'd had a great life, but he just had some regrets.

I thought for a moment and then nodded my head a little. At that, he was looking me right in the eyes. I would have been well within the rules of polite society to meander the conversation into more lighthearted fare. But I could tell he wanted a reaction. He wanted my thoughts on all that he had told me.

I'm not good at that.

I gave a good smile to my friend and said, "Man! Those ain't regrets! That's just baggage! We've all got it!"

I went on to talk about regrets and how we sometimes confuse them with the baggage that we all carry around. From the day we're born, we accumulate baggage. If you're over thirty, you have some. If you're over fifty, you've got the full set!

But regrets are not baggage. Life's baggage is inconvenient and trouble-some, but it has handles and wheels and rolls nicely along with you wherever you may go. It might slow you down, but it's manageable. You can dress it up with travel stickers and other proof of your existence. If done right, you can even brag about it and roll it out every once in a while for something to talk about. Baggage is bad grades on a test or tickets on your driving record. Even a stint in jail or a low credit score is just part of the baggage we accumulate.

Regrets are not baggage. Regrets are much darker. Regrets are invisible and have no handles or wheels. They're shaped like a two-hundred-pound anvil, and the only way to carry it is with both arms across your chest. You walk with it every waking hour, slunken over from its weight. You sit with it and try not to look exhausted while you carry on a conversation. At night, you sleep with it while trying to dream without its weight crushing your chest.

I know regrets. Regrets are not about choosing the wrong road. Regrets are about never even choosing a road. Regrets involve the deepest parts of our lives, like love and honor, pride and passion.

After my rambling explanation about baggage and regrets, I turned to my friend and asked him if he really thought that he had regrets.

He solemnly nodded yes.

At that moment, with the heaviness of the conversation squarely in the front of his mind, I saw in his face the dark burden of the heavy anvil. He didn't say what it was, and I didn't ask.

My own mind reminded me that I know a little about regrets. I had one, and I lugged it around for several years.

We had a few moments of silence. I watched in his face as his focusing thoughts added even more weight to the burden. I knew that whatever it was now swirled around in his mind. I silently wished that it had never even come up. I was angry with myself as I looked at my friend's wet eyes.

At that darkest moment of our conversation, I went on.

"Friend. There's something unique about regrets. Regrets are heavy, but they are like glass. You carry them, but at the same time, you protect them. But we too often fail to realize that the moment the burden is too much to bear, you can close your eyes, open your arms, and let them fall away. In an instant, they shatter on the ground. In that moment, you dust off the shards, walk away, and never look back."

I went on to talk about how our minds create them, but it's our decision to keep them.

My friend looked up at me with a hint of a smile.

"You're a good listener, Jones."

Then he stole one of my lines.

"And you're smarter than you look."

We both laughed. And laughter changed everything.

23

A Simple Choice

I n the early 1980s, I was a college student at the University of California, Davis. I entered as a junior, having completed two years at the community college in my hometown. College-town Davis was a culture shock, but I jumped in to acclimate as quickly as possible. I carried a blue leather backpack slung over one shoulder, rode my bicycle everywhere, and drank cappuccinos at the coffee houses downtown.

My scholastic life was a struggle. I had finished my community college with near-perfect grades. But university learning was on a whole new level. I sat in Chemistry classes and listened to lectures with five hundred other students. Some classes had almost as many students as the entire student body of my hometown college. I struggled with all of the math-based courses. UCD was on the quarter system, rather than the semester system that most other colleges followed. The quarter system meant that things happened fast. Physics, Calculus, and Statistics required three quarters each. If we add in the quarters of General Chemistry, Organic Chemistry, Environmental Toxicology, and a host of others, a poor farm boy like me was almost doomed.

If a student's GPA fell below 2.0 for a quarter, they would be put on academic probation. I lived on the dreaded AP. This is the university's way of putting the scarlet letter "F" on your forehead until you raise your grades. Two quarters in a row, and you would be expelled from the university. So, I quickly learned to stagger my classes. If I were on probation, I'd only take courses the next quarter where I knew I could excel. I'd get a 3.5 GPA that quarter, get off probation, and then start the whole process over. One quarter on. One quarter off. For me, it was a game of leapfrog, and I worked the system.

As bad as I was as a student, my campus life was a whole different matter. I loved it, and it loved me. As I walked around campus, there was an undeniable energy. You could feel the collective buzz of thousands of young people, learning, experimenting, pushing boundaries, and finding out who they really were. As much as I hated high school, I wanted to be on the university campus. I studied there. I ate lunch there. I drank beer there. I had friends there.

I was a few years older than most students but I had a boyish face. I had long hair and wore an Akubra Australian cowboy hat, so I stuck out more than most others. Campus life was my first adult opportunity to open up and really develop a love for people. I took full advantage of it. I took field trips to wildlife areas with the granola-ish crowd. I sat in the coffee houses and drank coffee with the PIBs (People In Black). I played hacky-sack in the quad with the skater crowd, and I played in drum circles with the hippies. I even studied at night with giggling sorority girls. I loved all of them, and they loved me back.

After only my first quarter, I could walk most anywhere on campus and get hollered at. "Hey Rawge, where you going?" I'd walk somewhere for lunch and hear, "Hey Rawge, we're over here." On one beautiful spring day, I was walking through campus with my backpack on my shoulder when I stopped to let an open-air tour bus pass. The bus stopped in the little campus street in front of me, and the tour guide hollered on the speaker, "Hey Rawge, come talk to us!" I stepped onto the bus, took the microphone, and gave a five-minute impromptu campus life speech to a bus full of energetic high school seniors.

As shy as I was about speaking to groups, I somehow managed to become an unofficial student spokesman for my wildlife biology major. I confidently spoke at a fund-raising dinner, addressed the freshman class, and was interviewed by the college paper. I was truly living the campus life!

But somewhere in there, the fun and façade of notoriety took a toll. It was imperceptible to me, but it was there. Just a little bit of the shine and glimmer of popularity took something away from me and who I was. I didn't even realize it was gone, and I wouldn't have known what it was. But like almost anything you lose, you don't miss it until you need it.

During spring break of my senior year, I was working in northern California as a fish biologist aide. It was a cool job. My friend Craig and I would hike along streams all day with big backpacks full of gear and food. Following a map, we would stop at prescribed spots and snorkel through a one-hundred-meter stretch of river and identify and count the fish living in that stretch of water. At night, we would camp, cook, roll out our sleeping bags, and live on the banks of the river. I spent my days in shorts, hiking boots, and no shirt. It seemed to be a dream job. All that and a paycheck!

After a few weeks of work, we would drive back to Davis to spend a few days at home. I lived in an apartment on Eighth Street, across from an old strip mall. The mall had a big supermarket, a bagel shop, a jewelry store, and other random places to spend your money. I shopped in the supermarket but I mostly lived off the bargain day-old bagels from the bagel shop.

On Saturday after getting home, I'd walked across the street to the supermarket. After being gone for three weeks, there wasn't much that was edible in my refrigerator. I'd walk over in shorts, a tank top, and flip-flops. I was tan from head to toe and in the best physical shape of my life. I walked with my head up. I was Rawge, and I had it going on!

One particularly memorable Saturday of shopping, I gathered my few items in a basket and headed to the checkout. There were only two lanes open, and one was a few people shorter than the other. I took the short line. As I stood there looking around, a stench caught my nose. In front of me was an old drunk, covered in filth. No wonder the other line was so long. His dirty pants were sagging, and he used one hand at a belt loop to pretend to hold them up. Even as he tried to keep his pants up, they sagged enough for me to see several inches of stained brown underwear that was supposed to be white. Of course, the other hand held a bottle of cheap wino wine. I was disgusted.

This was a family store. Surely, there's a cheap liquor store he could have gone to. I shouldn't have to hold my nose to check out in a grocery store. I looked over at the other line. It still had more people in it, but I moved over anyway. I'd suffer through a few extra minutes, so I didn't have to stand behind the dirty old drunk.

After a minute or two, the clerk checked out my items and returned them to me in a neat brown paper bag. I picked it up, said thank you, and walked to the door. As I got into the sunlight, I saw the old drunk in front of me, shuffling his feet and tugging at his pants with a free finger. I stopped to watch just as his finger slipped, and his baggy pants fell all the way below his knees. He couldn't even bend down to pick them up, so he stood there looking around and then continued shuffling his feet with his pants at his ankles. I just shook my head and veered at an angle so I didn't have to pass by him.

As I looked around to see if anyone was judging me for avoiding him, a young college girl, about twenty years old, ran over to him. I had seen her around the apartments and traded pleasantries. She knelt down at the old man's feet and slowly wriggled his pants back up to his waist. The young girl used her own hand to hold the pants up and put her free hand on his shoulder. As she talked to him, he pointed to a bus bench on the sidewalk, and the two of them headed in that direction. It was a slow walk as the old man shuffled his feet in small steps. I watched until they reached the bench. The old drunk sat down, and she sat beside him. She stayed to talk with the old guy as I walked by to cross the street.

When I reached my apartment, I busted through my door and threw my bag on the kitchen table. I walked a few more steps and sat in a huff on my little couch in the dark living room. I was so ashamed of myself. That young gal had convicted me! My mind reeled. What had happened to me? When did I become a soulless man with a good tan? A pretty young girl had more compassion in her little finger than I had in my whole body.

There have been plenty of times in my life, even chapters in this very book, when I was ashamed. There were plenty of times when I had let myself down. But none of them equaled this moment. None of the others moved me to tears. I sat in the dark for over an hour. Before I stood up, I silently prayed for compassion.

Now, I didn't walk outside the next day, just beaming with compassion. I didn't wake up as Mother Teresa's intern. Nope. Compassion would come slowly. I felt I had to develop it. It would take time.

Some years later, though, I learned that compassion is not something you're born with, lose, gain, or develop—rather, it is quite simply something you choose to allow in your life.

I choose compassion.

24

Just Do Something

I was watching an old war movie, and somewhere during a lull in a battle, the protagonist said, "I can't just sit here anymore. I'm gonna do something." So he grabbed his pistol, stood up, and headed into the battlefield, guns blazing. He walked right past several soldiers and shot the cannon soldier. He shot five or six others, then went on to shoot five or six more. He almost single-handedly won the battle. All while his comrades watched safely from their foxholes. During the battle, he never received as much as a scratch!

Okay, that's Hollywood. Nowhere in time has that ever happened. In the movie, he was impervious to bullets, sabers, and cannon balls, all because he decided to "do something." The problem is that it leaves us with a not-so-subtle message that heroes just go for it. Us wimps, we wait.

A few weeks ago, I was stuck in traffic. About once or twice a week, I end up sitting on I-5 at J Street. I stop, go twenty feet, stop, then go twenty feet again. Pretty soon, the "go twenty feet part" goes away. Then it's just sit.

On this day, after we'd been sitting for a few minutes, I saw the guy behind me pull into the emergency lane and go. As he passed by me, I could almost read his lips, "I can't just sit here anymore. I'm gonna do something." Well, I saw him again about a mile up the road, with a trooper leaning into his window and giving him a fat ticket. This ain't Hollywood.

Last week, I was stopped in traffic at the same spot. I was tired and irritated and just wanted to get home. I looked left and right to see if I could get into another lane so maybe I could inch up. I was just about to be "that guy" and do something. But I heard a siren, and cops and emergency vehicles started passing me in the emergency lane. Hmm... I settled down for a minute.

My Dad used to be fond of saying, "Do something, even if it's wrong!"

Well, there's a bit of validity to that under certain circumstances. The problem is that I don't have nearly the discernment to decide which are the proper circumstances. My life has proven that many times.

I've come to realize, that much of our lives are going to be spent waiting. It sucks, but it's just part of life. We wait for our dinner at a restaurant. We wait at the Department of Motor Vehicles, swearing that every employee is on snail drugs. We wait in lines at the store. We wait for checks in the mail. And yes, we wait in traffic.

So, I sat back and decided to do something. I bumped the bass on my sub up a notch and turned up some music.

A mere twenty seconds later, my blood pressure was back down. About twenty seconds after that, my heart rate was down. And guess what? About twenty seconds after that, I was chill. I wasn't moving, but I was chill.

When fighting a battle with gray hair, wrinkles, and high blood pressure, sometimes "just do something" takes on a whole new meaning.

25

My Rescue Story

I've heard it asked many times, "Are you a dog person or a cat person?" Unequivocally, I'm a dog person! I love dogs. I tolerate cats pretty well, but I'd take a dog's genuineness over a cat's arrogance any day.

I've had a dog for most of my life. When I was a very small kid, I had an adorable mutt, named Jeremiah. This was back when that bullfrog song was so popular. The dog was about knee-high, had shaggy fur, and a tail that curled in a circle. He was a good friend. He listened to me well, or at least as well as I listened to my folks. But as is the case with most farm dogs, he didn't have a long life. I cried. I missed my friend. A month or two after that *friend* position opened up, Dad brought home a little brown dog named Chico. This was my new buddy! This was the kind of friend that was open to anything, from jumping into the boxcar of a train to climbing a wooden ladder up to a tree fort. Every kid needs a dog like Chico.

When I was older and more into horses and cattle, I got my first cow dog. He was half Australian Kelpie and half Queensland Heeler. His name was Jake, and I got him as an unruly half-grown pup. I saw him not long after he was born, up in the hills on a working cattle ranch. My friend owned the ranch, and I was helping him for the day. On the drive back down to town in his Jeep, we stopped by a little cabin so he could show me the pups. As soon as we parked, a bunch of little wiggling bodies ran out from under the porch. I picked each one up and played with it for a few minutes. I sat in the shade, and the puppies just climbed all over me. They were happy to see someone in their secluded home.

As I sat and tried to give each pup some attention, I saw a pair of eyes looking from under the darkness of the wooden porch steps. I looked over to my friend. He told me that pup wasn't very friendly and hardly ever came out to play. I crawled closer, stuck out my hand, and wiggled my fingers in the universal symbol of friendliness. The black pup just growled a little.

A few months later, I was back at the ranch for a day to help round up some calves. As we passed the cabin, I asked about the pups. Teddy told me that they were all gone, except for the black one. It was mean, and no one wanted it. I asked if we could go see it.

Just as last time, we pulled under a shade tree in front of the cabin. As the Jeep idled in, I watched the half-grown pup squeeze back under the porch. I got out and walked closer. My friend told me his name was Jake. I walked closer, sat down, and patted my knee.

"Come on, boy. Come on out, Jake"

At my words, the one-foot-tall black pup bolted from under the porch and jumped into my lap. In a second, it was licking my fingers, whining, and wiggling its whole body from excitement.

"Well," my friend said, "I guess he's yours." And he *was* mine. Or maybe *I* was his. Either way, for the next fourteen years, we were nearly inseparable. He rode in my truck, in the front seat on the highways, or in the truck's bed on the dirt roads. He never needed a leash and would stay one foot from my feet as we walked. It seemed that he could speak English and knew everything I needed from him. He could push cattle in a chute or get in front and lead a snorting bull into a trailer. And as a bonus, if he sensed any trouble with someone, he'd stand a foot in front of me and growl.

Since then, I've had other dogs—Doc, a registered Australian Cattle dog, and most recently, Moon, a half Queensland Heeler and half Border Collie. Yes, I am a dog person!

One day recently, I was hanging around inside our little neighborhood store, chatting with the owner, the friendliest guy in town. I always stand to the side so he can wait on customers, and we talk in between. As we chatted, a lady walked in, clutching a small black dog with one arm. When she got close, I looked the dog over. It was jet black, had short hair, and was not much bigger than a Chihuahua. My mind traveled back a few decades. I think I know that dog!

I asked the lady about her armful of black fur. She jumped right in and told me the dog's life story. She told me a somewhat well-rehearsed speech of how she rescued it and slowly coaxed it out of a host of bad habits. She explained how she had paid hundreds in vet bills to get it healthy and went into detail about every diagnosis. The lady held up its paws and told me that she was going next door to get its nails trimmed. She went on and on. Those stories are important, and God bless everyone who has ever adopted an unwanted animal. But her story was a little long. When she finally finished, I asked her this question. "What kind of dog is it?" I braced for a particular answer.

"I don't know. Just a mutt, I guess."

After her fifteen-minute rescue story, that answer was a letdown.

I knew exactly what kind of dog it was.

A long time ago, I lived in a small town on the west side of the San Joaquin Valley. It was everything anyone could imagine about a small town. Everyone knew everyone. Everybody was related to somebody. And there was never much to do. I wasn't much older than the legal drinking age, and I was married to my first wife, Robin. She was a wonderful woman, and she was also a dog person. And a cat person. Well, she was an animal person. When it came to animals, whether birds, mammals, or anything in between, she had a huge heart.

Since there was never much to do in our little town, my friends and I were always open to anything new that came on the scene. In 1984, something unique was happening in the Santa Cruz and Marin County mountains. People were taking clunker cruiser bikes and modifying them for off-road riding. Mountain biking was born, and we were in.

Before long, my closest friends and I had our bikes. Fifteen gears, a big fat tire in the front, and a smaller fat tire in the back. The area around my hometown proved to be perfect for this new sport. There were steep hills just a few minutes to the west and dry creek beds a few minutes to the east. Every evening after work or every weekend, we found ourselves somewhere on our bikes.

The hills required us to pile the bikes into the back of a truck and then squeeze several grown men into the cab for a ten-minute drive. But we could hit the creek beds straight from our bikes. We'd all meet up at the Liquor Store parking lot at the edge of town. Then we'd pedal over the Warthan Creek bridge and dive off the highway onto a little dirt road. A quarter mile in, we'd steer into the creek bed, and then our world was wide open.

The short ride on the dirt road took us past the city's dog pound. It wasn't much more than a shed and about a dozen wire pens, each with a little plywood doghouse in the corner. The whole mess was surrounded by a six-foot-high chain-link fence with a locked gate.

As we zipped by in the dirt, every dog in the place would bark. Some of the barks were loud and deep, signaling the presence of the big dogs. Others were high and yappy, the verbal calling card of the little dogs.

Occasionally we'd stop and take a break at the dog pound, to the delight of the lonesome dogs. The entrance gate had a big chain and lock and an even bigger and official-looking sign that told the exact criminal offense and the potential maximum penalty for illegally entering. None of us were as respectful of the law back then as we are today, so we'd occasionally climb over the fence and have a look. Our ease with flaunting the law was bolstered by the fact that one of our biker gang's uncles was the dogcatcher. There was a general agreement that if it ever hit the fan, my friend Rick could talk our way out of trouble.

As we'd walk from pen to pen, every dog would bark, wag their tail, and stick their nose and tongue through the wire. We'd pet them and talk to them one by one. We had convinced ourselves they had all escaped from their backyards and had gotten picked up by the dogcatcher. The moment their absence was noticed, their owners would be quick to come down, pay their ransom, and take them home. It must have been true, to some degree, as each time we visited, there was a brand new crop of barking fuzzy noses.

One cool evening, we hopped over the fence as we were returning from a ride. We went down the row of barking noses. Every one of them looked dirty and mutt-ish, but we still gave each one some attention. At the last pen, there was a little black dog with a short, clean, shiny black coat. The little thing didn't bark but stood at the edge of the wire, looking up at me. Whatever it was, it had beautiful, attentive eyes and a stare that spoke more than a bark. Its ears stood up at the sound of my voice, yet it still didn't make a sound. It didn't seem afraid. It just seemed like a dog that felt like keeping its distance. We all looked at and spoke to it, and then we talked about what a cool-looking dog it was.

As we chatted, every dog suddenly stopped barking and looked towards the gate. Even our own ears perked up as we heard a car coming in the distance. In a moment, we high-tailed it back over the fence and regained the safety of the dirt road and our bikes.

A few days later, we revisited the pound. Some of the dogs were gone, but the beautiful little black dog was still there. It was there again a few days later and again a few days after that. Each time we visited, we talked about the unique little black dog and wondered when its owners would arrive to pick it up.

A week went by, and we were all too busy to ride. One evening, my friend Rick called me on the phone. He told me that he had spoken to his uncle, the dogcatcher. In the conversation, Rick mentioned the black dog and was told it was scheduled to be sent away the next day to be put down. As soon as Rick finished being roundly scolded by his uncle for trespassing at the city dog facility, he hung up and called me with the bad news.

None of us saw that coming. We'd have to do something. Robin and I had three dogs, and the last thing we needed was another one. I asked Rick if he could take it. Nope, out of the question. We scratched our heads to think of anyone else who might want it, but we came up with no one. As a last resort, I asked Rick if he could meet me at the pound in an hour. He agreed, and within one spin of the clock dial, we were scaling the dog-pound fence.

There were only two dogs there that day, a big hound with jingly tags hanging from its collar and the little black dog. Each gate had a lock, but the chain-link fence was held on with metal clips and wire. I had a multi-tool in

159

a little pack that hung below my mountain bike seat. In under five minutes, we had a tiny corner of the fence pulled back and were trying to coax the little black thing into our hands. From this close perspective, we could see that it was a girl. So, we started calling every girl name we could think of.

"Come on, Betsy. Here, here, Bella. Hey girl, hey Daisy. Come on Zoe, Come on Molly."

We tried a hundred different names. And then I said, "Come here, Nikki." At that, the little thing walked over, wiggled through the crack in the fence, and was in my arms. Rick and I quietly cheered. I scrambled back over the fence, Rick handed me the dog, and then he crawled over the wire. We had no plan, but the little thing was no longer in the pound. I told him I would just take her home and play it by ear. I'd explain the situation to Robin and hope for the best.

I rode my bike home with one hand on the handlebars and the other cradling a few pounds of nervous dog. Once home, I put the little thing down in our living room while the other three dogs looked through the back door glass. None of them seemed overly alarmed at the intruder. Nikki walked around, sniffing and checking the place out. Even Robin's cat didn't seem to mind.

Robin had been twenty miles up in the hills, visiting her folks. I sat down and hadn't even gotten comfortable when she came through the door. Nikki ran straight to her and sat down just inches from her feet.

Robin tossed her keys on a table and got a big smile on her face. "Well, who are you, little thing?"

She reached down, scooped up the black bundle, and then looked at me.

"Her name is Nikki, and me and Rick broke her out of the dog pound. They were gonna put her down!" I blurted out as quickly as I could say it. I hadn't had time to develop a better story, or lie, or something that might be more palatable. The truth would just have to do.

And then I blurted out, "I'm pretty sure she's a purebred Ethiopian Weasel Hound!" Robin just gave me a disgusted look, knowing I had made that up, and turned back to nuzzling the new family member.

Nikki became hers and soon paid little attention to me. She walked ahead of us on a little leash when we took evening walks. Most everyone we passed would comment about its beautiful black fur or her dazzling eyes. Rob would just shake her head when I'd tell people that her name was Nikki and that she was a purebred Ethiopian Weasel Hound. It seemed believable. I'd always have a grin when people would respond with comments like, "Oh, I love that breed!" or sometimes, "Yes, I've heard some great things about them!"

Okay, that's my rescue story, and it's longer than the story I complained about from the lady at the market. I hope I see her again sometime. She needs to know what a prize she carries around. She needs to know that she's one of only two people in the world who have ever rescued a purebred Ethiopian Weasel Hound!

On an ending note, does anyone know the statute of limitations for breaking into a city facility and stealing a dog?

Asking for a friend!

26

The Forty-Year Lesson

S ome people know and understand great things. They can think bigger than they are. They see a world that is bigger than us. Some of them are powerful and influential and can put their knowledge and abilities to great use. These people can change the course of the world and leave it a better place.

Some great thinkers are less powerful and less influential. Some of them are farmers with a fourth-grade education. They can't use their wide-thinking abilities to change the course of the world. But they can use it to change the world of a ten-year-old boy.

In the 1930s, California began building the Central Valley Project. This massive endeavor consisted of a series of twenty dams and reservoirs, eleven electrical power plants, over five hundred miles of major canals, and a host of ancillary conduits, tunnels, and other facilities. The colossal project manages over nine million acre-feet of water and provides water to one-third of California's agriculture, the backbone of our economy. The project generates enough electricity to provide for two-million people. This massive multi-decade project helped California become the world's fifth-largest economy.

In 1963, the project began construction of the California Aqueduct. This four-hundred-and-forty-four-mile canal stretches from the Sacramento-San Joaquin Delta in the north to the Tehachapi mountains in the south. The meandering waterway parallels Interstate 5, winding right through the San

Joaquin Valley.

When I was a kid, none of that meant anything to me other than the canal was serendipitously dug just a few miles from our house. It seemed like it took forever to be built as we detoured around the construction every time we drove into our little town of Huron. I was only five or six, but I stared out the window every time we passed by. I asked a lot of questions about it, but really, all I cared about was one thing. When it's full, will it have fish in it?

I was closer to ten years old when it was finally completed and filled. And yes, it did have fish in it. At first, the only fish were the few that had entered from the Delta. But after a few years, those fish spawned in the canal, and it became a regular fishing spot. It was a four-hundred-mile-long fishing hole, and I was lucky enough to have it built almost in my backyard.

I loved to go fishing in the canal. The water had the usual array of fish that I was familiar with, like bass, bluegill, and catfish, but it introduced a new fish to the valley residents—the striped bass. This fish was native to the East Coast but had been introduced into the California Delta. This eastern expat found a home and thrived in the new canal. We called them stripers. Even as a kid, I caught a couple that were bigger than I could hold up for a Polaroid picture. A week didn't go by without someone walking around our farm and bragging about a twenty-pounder or thirty-pounder they had caught. By 1970, the words "striper" and "canal" were on every young Huron boy's mind.

My dad was always busy on the farm but he did like to fish. So, whenever he had a few free hours, he would take my brother Steve and me to the canal. We had a spot about halfway between the bridge at Gale Avenue and the "Gates," a series of mechanical devices that controlled the flow of the water. The area was peaceful. It was far enough from the bridge that passing cars couldn't see us. My dad knew everyone in the surrounding forty miles, so if we were too close, every passing car or truck honked their horn to say hello. The halfway point was perfect, and we had proven that the fish loved it there, too.

Occasionally, on days when Steve was away with friends, Dad would ask if I wanted to go fishing. It was somewhat of a rhetorical question. Without an answer, I'd run and start gathering up our gear. Two fishing poles, a tackle box, a long-handled net, and a frozen bag of anchovies for bait. The cold anchovies would get wrapped tightly in a plastic bag before they went into a little cooler so the smelly fish didn't foul up his six-pack of Coors.

Fishing at the canal was mostly just sitting. After we got our lines baited and cast out as far as we could throw them, we set the poles into little holders that Dad had built out of metal pipe and rebar. We tightened up the lines and then sat back and watched the tips of the poles, just waiting for a bite. When the tip bent down, we jumped up, grabbed the pole, set the hook, and started reeling. Of course, that was the fun part. The sitting and watching was just boring. But that's the part that Dad liked the most.

Pops didn't talk a lot. He didn't idly chat or gossip. He didn't talk just for the sake of talking. When he talked, there was a purpose behind it. He was leading up to something. He wanted me to think about something. He wanted to teach me something. But a big lesson was usually hidden behind a small question.

I, on the other hand, just liked to talk. I dominated the one-sided *conversations*. "I wonder how many fish are in here? Did you know that fish lay eggs? Wouldn't it be cool if a whale came down the canal? You know there's whales up where it starts. The lady in the library showed me a map." *Blah, blah, blah*, I chattered.

One day, I mentioned that I was glad they had built a bridge for us. That sentence was Dad's key to jump in.

"What if they didn't? How could we build a bridge across to the other side? You and I, how would we build it?"

I didn't know it at that moment, but that question started a month-long conversation. I also didn't know that the full meaning wouldn't really sink in for another forty years.

I rattled off an answer about a pair of steel pipes stretched across to the other side and wooden boards screwed in between them. Or maybe even steel angle-iron bolted in for strength.

Dad asked me how far it was to the other side.

I took a guess. "Seventy-five or a hundred feet."

He told me that the Gale Avenue bridge was one hundred and four feet wide and that further upstream, the canal was one hundred and ten feet wide. But he stressed that we couldn't work from a guess at our building point. We needed to be sure. We certainly didn't want it to break in half and drown us both the first time we tried to cross.

Then Pops started analyzing. He told me that we probably couldn't build it alone. First, we would need surveyors. He went on to explain in detail what surveyors can do. He told me how they used lines, math, and trigonometry to determine precise distances and locations. He explained about their equipment, like the transit I had seen them peering through but had never understood its purpose. We talked about surveyors for an hour or more.

When it was time to go home, he asked me to keep thinking about the bridge. I was always a deal maker, so I assured him that I would if we could come back to this spot again, alone next week. Dad put his own demands into the deal. He would not forget, so I wasn't to pester him about bringing me back. Not a word. I nodded yes, and we clinched the deal with a grin and a handshake.

For the next week, I thought about the bridge and made plans. I sketched it in my bedside notebook. I pictured it in my mind and came up with questions. I would be more prepared during our next fishing trip.

A week or so later, just as promised, Dad said let's go fishing. I hustled up our gear, and we drove back to our spot. We got set up, got our poles baited, and cast out into the water. The moment we were both sitting comfortably on the bank, he asked me what I came up with.

I rattled off my plan. Once the surveyors told us how far it was across, we'd use the pipes I mentioned last time, cut them to the correct length, and drag them across. I filled in some other details and then looked at Pops for his reply.

"Okay, what diameter and how thick are the pipes? We want to make sure they will hold us. We don't want it to break in half and drown us the first time we use it."

Of course, I was stumped. So, Pops told me that we would have to enlist the help of engineers. He told me how engineers use science and testing to understand the strength of materials. They know steel, wood, concrete, and most any other material. They understand forces, distances, leverage, and other factors that affect the ability of materials to safely perform a function.

We left that day with the same deal. I'd keep plotting the bridge, I wouldn't pester Dad, and we'd return in a week or so.

Dad kept his promise, and each week, I learned more about what is involved in building something useful, safe, and long-lasting. One of the more shocking moments to me was when we seemed to have a bridge that would function, but then Pops told me that it would surely be ugly. He mentioned the word aesthetics. He told me that it needed to be as beautiful as it was functional and that we would need to bring in some artists to help make it look nice. Further, we would need someone to write something profound and beautiful for a plaque at the entrance. He finished by telling me the next time I was in that library that I loved so much, to find a picture of the beautiful Golden Gate Bridge in San Francisco or the Tower drawbridge in our own state capital in Sacramento.

By the end of summer, we had caught a dozen fish and had developed a plan for a hypothetical bridge. But to do it justice, the scribbled notes in my little notebook said that we would require surveyors, architects, engineers, scientists, artists, painters, welders, carpenters, mathematicians, poets, and a host of others. I'm surprised that he didn't throw in a philosopher or two!

And all I really wanted was to fish with my dad and have him all to myself.

By the time school rolled back around, I didn't think much about building a bridge, but I never looked at another one the same. No matter where we went, I pointed out the bridges that we crossed. Big, little and in-between. Some of them I marveled at, and others I offered the profound criticism I gained from my new knowledge. I was especially tough on the ugly ones.

We stopped the truck once after crossing a little concrete bridge after I had deemed it ugly. The bridge wasn't very big and crossed over a small creek. Dad wanted to show me a stamp in the concrete. We walked down below the road until we could see the thick concrete columns. In bold letters about four inches tall, the stamp read "WPA 1941." He explained to me how the Work Projects Administration had given jobs to millions of out-of-work men during the Great Depression. He mentioned that even my Papa Kinley had worked for them. He chuckled that maybe Papa had built the ugly bridge. I looked it over again and confessed that it wasn't as ugly as I had first thought.

Since then, I've seen many bridges, from masterpieces like the beautiful Sundial in Redding, California, and the little gothic Pont De Bisbe Bridge in Barcelona, Spain, to barely passable rope suspension bridges in Panama. I've thought about them all.

Almost forty years after Pops and I *built* the canal bridge, Rhonda and I were in Pisa, Italy. We walked streets full of great art and strolled through the same cobblestone alleys where the world's greatest architects, scientists, astronomers, and mathematicians had once walked.

While there and learning the city's intellectual history, I had an amazing realization—four hundred and fifty years earlier, Fibonacci, Galileo, Michelangelo, da Vinci, Botticelli, Brunelleschi, Caravaggio, Vasari, Pontormo, and Rosso Fiorentino were all in the same city at the exact same time! Our world would not be the same today if not for their immeasurable contributions! Clearly, the powerful Medici family knew the strength of paying artists, architects, and scientists!

As we strolled the narrow streets, I silently thought about Mr. Cosimo di Giovanni de' Medici, the ruler of all of Florence during the Italian Renaissance. Was this generous patron of the Arts, Science, Learning, and Architecture, trying to change the world? Or was he simply gathering enough brilliant professionals to build a safe, beautiful, and functional bridge? Either way, he knew how to assemble a crew.

My lesson was finally complete.

27

That Still Small Voice

W hen I don't fully understand something, I've always jokingly said, "I don't understand all I know about it but..." And then I state what I know.

I've always liked the idea of intuition. Maybe there's actually something that speaks to us and guides us a bit—something that we don't understand. What I call God, you might call instinct or a sixth sense or something like that. Whatever words we choose, I think there is something to it.

I found a picture on my phone that reminded me of a time about ten years ago, when that voice talked to me.

I was at work, and for a few days, I had been working on writing a complicated report. I'm a wildlife biologist on a nature area. I'm supposed to spend my time outdoors. But I had been pinned to my desk and computer screen for a little too long.

One afternoon, I just needed a break. My computer screen was full of spreadsheets, documents, and pages of text I had written. Then, in all of my mess, I'd managed to lose a reference document somewhere, and I was about ready to scream and pull my hair out. So, I stood up, frustrated, and said to no one, "I'm going outside for a walk."

I opened the office door and made my way outside. The air was better, but there was construction going on all around us, and vehicles seemingly in every direction. So I decided that I'd just drive around the refuge for a few minutes and clear my head.

I started my pickup truck and then had to decide where to go. I was literally in the middle of twenty-five hundred acres of wetlands, oak woodlands, and riparian forests. I could drive in any compass direction.

Here's where that small voice comes in. For no explainable reason, I decided to drive a short distance to our old office site. The old buildings had been torn down and there wasn't much left out there. It's not pretty or peaceful, and to get there, I would have to get out and open a couple of large security gates held closed with rusty locks. I could drive to most any other part of the refuge without ever having to leave my truck. But I didn't. I pointed my truck towards the ugly old office site.

Once I drove inside the deserted yard, I parked my truck and walked straight to the few trees that were still growing in the back. When we moved out, we had left a few pallets of junk piled below them. It was stuff that we still occasionally needed, but it hadn't even been looked at for a year or two.

I stood for a minute and looked up in the trees. There were no birds or squirrels, so I looked down at the pallets, overgrown with weeds. My scanning eyes stopped at a big wooden spool of plastic pipe just a couple of feet from my legs. It was the type of wooden spool that people would re-purpose into patio tables and other things. It wasn't a big one, but it was about two feet tall and about just as wide.

As I looked it over, I was startled to see a little face staring at me from the small center hole in the spool. It took a few seconds for my mind to tell me what I was seeing. But there in front of me was a kitten with panic in its eyes. The poor thing was stuck in the hole in the middle of the spool!

When I leaned over for a closer look, all it could muster was a frantic hiss and a wiggle that would just spin its dangling body in circles. No matter what it did, its head was too big to fall back through the spool. I could see it had been there long enough to wear off a ring of hair around its neck.

I hustled back to my truck to see what I might locate to attempt to free the poor little desperate critter. I rummaged around and managed to find a big screwdriver. I hoped that I could use it to split open the top of the wooden spool enough for the helpless critter to drop out. Through hissing

172

and spinning, just a few inches from my hand, I wedged the screwdriver into a small crack and gave a quick pull. The old spool was just rotten enough for it to work, and the little kitty dropped back into the spool, out of sight.

The hole in the spool was covered with kitty hair, but I hoped the little creature was okay. With both hands and some effort, I turned the spool over onto its side. I was happy to watch the little animal amble off and disappear into the other junk scattered around the trees.

I returned to the old office site a few days later. As I approached the area quietly, I saw the little kitty sitting with its sibling and staring at me. It was fine.

I wondered how long the little feline ball of fur had hung there in the heat, without food or water. I knew that it certainly would have died had I not freed it from the spool's grasp.

For the next week or so, I thought about that day. I hadn't been to that spot for months and I wouldn't return for months afterwards. But on that day, at that hour, I drove there like I was on a mission. That cute kitty was alive because of that little voice that said, "Listen to me Rawge. Follow me Rawge. Go there Rawge."

I don't understand all I know about it, but...maybe there is something to it. That small voice may be speaking to you today. You may hear it saying, "Go buy Rawge's other book."

Okay, that was actually *my* voice.

And now it's telling me, "Always end funny, Rawge. You're not a good enough writer yet to end profoundly!"

28

The Hunderds

I like the word *hundred*. I like it even more when I change the end from
"red" to "erd." It just sounds cool. A hunderd bucks. A hunderd pounds.
A hunderd miles.

I remember a day that came up all hunderds.

About thirty-five years ago, I was in college and working for a state senator
who had a little gentleman's farm. A gentleman's farm is almost like a real
farm, except it's for rich people who want to tell their friends that they own
a farm. I didn't care. It was a good gig. There was always something that
needed doing, so I could just drive over anytime I didn't have a class, and
go to work. The senator would show up at some point and pay me cash. It
worked out great.

One Thursday evening, the senator called me and told me he was in a jam
and asked if I could work on Friday. I told him that I had classes on Friday,
but if it were really necessary, I'd meet him in the morning and work, but
that I'd have to leave for a few hours to attend class. Afterward, I could return
and work the rest of the day. He told me that was fine and we'd meet the
next morning at five o'clock a.m. That was early for a gentleman farmer, so I
figured it must be serious.

I was there the next morning as the sun came up, anxious to see what was
so important. It was going to be hot, so I had a milk jug full of cold water and a
sandwich. Just as agreed, the senator drove up and motioned for me to follow

him. I drove my truck and followed the senator over to a remote spot on the farm. It only took a minute for me to see the problem. There was a big trailer loaded with bags of concrete sitting in some mud. Even worse, the trailer had a broken axle. Another trailer was sitting nearby, but well away from the wet ground. The senator explained that he needed all the concrete bags moved over to the empty trailer. I asked him how many bags. One hundred. I asked him how heavy they were. One hundred pounds. I'm no math whiz, but it only took me a minute to respond.

"Damn, that's five tons!"

He said, "I know, but it's got to be moved so I can get the trailer out and to the repair shop. It's a lot, but I can get a crew of guys here from another farm for an hour or so while you're gone back to school. They should get a bunch of it done, and then you can finish it when you get back after school."

Oh well, it all pays the same, so I got started. I'd grab a bag, get it positioned, then walk over to the other trailer and drop it off. The bags were heavy, but the work wouldn't kill me. It was cool, and after a few trips, it was just a routine. Grab a bag, get it over my shoulder, and start walking.

Soon, though, I started doing what I always do when I'm bored. I started counting stuff. I count birds or clouds or trees or most anything I can find. On that day, I counted steps. After another trip or two, I realized that it was one hundred steps round trip. I quit counting and started thinking... Hmm. Interesting. I'm moving one hundred bags, weighing one hundred pounds, for one hundred steps.

I mulled the odd pattern over for a while and then got back to the back-breaking work. After a bit, I needed a break and a drink of water. I walked over to my truck and opened the door. I leaned back with my jug of water and turned on the truck's radio. I was listening to an AM station that played country music. I didn't like the DJ much, but the station came in good. The DJ talked too much and never played two songs back-to-back without a bunch of talking in between. I caught the last half of Rosanne Cash singing *"Tennessee Flat Top Box"* and then the blabbering DJ started in talking again. He started talking about a big celebration that was happening in Guntersville, Alabama. Apparently, the entire town had shown up to help a pair of twin sisters celebrate their one-hundredth birthday!

I grinned and shook my head at the news. Of course, it was a centennial birthday party. Another hunderd in my day. A hunderd bags weighing a hunderd pounds for a hunderd steps, while a couple of old ladies celebrate their hunderdth birthday. Hmm. Funny weird.

I drank my water and got back to work. At 10:30, I jumped in my truck to head to school. I needed a shower but didn't have time. I'd have to rely on my 24-hr deodorant to keep me on good terms with the other students. In the parking lot, I pulled off my t-shirt with cut-off sleeves and put on something more appropriate for school. I hurried over to the building and got me a seat.

I listened to the professor, took my notes, and a couple of hours later, I was back at the gentleman's farm.

When I pulled up, I was delighted to see that a crew had actually shown up while I was gone and had made a huge dent in the pile of bags. I looked it over for a minute and then realized the rest of the heavy bags weren't gonna move themselves, so I dug back in and started making round trips to the trailer. It didn't take long before my back started to ache, and I realized that it wasn't nearly as easy as it was in the morning. Besides being tired, it had gotten hot. I was wiping sweat from my face when I heard some noise from the road, and the senator rolled up in his fancy golf cart. His wife had made a big glass of cold iced tea for me. I wished for a moment that she had brought it. She was terribly pretty, but moreover, she was sweet to a fault. I always enjoyed talking with her about horses or home. Before she married the senator, she was from a town not far from where I grew up. I wasn't surprised that she sent me a cold drink.

The senator handed me the tea and mentioned that it looked like I'd get the trailer finished in an hour or two. He said he'd be back to pay me. Before he drove off, he told me to make sure I drank plenty of water. He said that he'd just left the barn and the thermometer said it was exactly one hundred degrees.

Again, I shook my head. Of course, it was one hundred degrees. It just wouldn't be right if it were ninety-nine or one hundred and one. Today, it's all about them hunderds!

A couple of hours later, I dropped the last bag on the trailer. I stretched my arms a few times and wiggled my shoulders to try and shake off some of the aches. I walked to my truck and sat down to cool off. I started the truck and turned the air conditioner to max. The old truck was about worn out, but in a minute or so, I felt some cool air on my face. As I sat, gunning the engine a little to try and coax some colder air, and thinking over the day's events, the senator's golf cart came around the corner. I pulled my truck forward a little to get it in the shade of an oak tree and got out. The senator hopped out of his rig and thanked me for helping him out of a jam. He opened his wallet and handed me four twenty-dollar bills. As I reached for it, I inadvertently let out a chuckle. It was an accident. Yes, of course, I was expecting a hundred, but without all the day's weird phenomena, I certainly wouldn't have laughed at eighty bucks.

The senator wrinkled his face and looked at me. "Is that not enough?"

"No, that's plenty!" I said with a hint of embarrassment at my inappropriately timed chortle.

"Well damn, here then!"

He put the 4 twenties back in his wallet and handed me a crisp hundred.

I couldn't help but get a big grin as I took it from his hand. The senator laughed for a second and then jumped back in his cart.

"Thanks again. See ya next week," and he drove off.

I couldn't help but laugh a few more times on my drive home. I thought about all the hundreds and the pattern. I thought it most interesting that the pattern was so strong that when it was almost broken, it fixed itself. The pattern made me chuckle at a very improper moment, but it fixed the pattern. I reasoned that something was going on, and it was powerful! I wondered, now what? How could I harness this new-found phenomenon? Could I get rich on the lottery? Nope. It doesn't even have a hundred numbers. Keno? Nope. Bingo? Nope. Blackjack? Not even close.

I thought about it hard for the rest of my drive. There has to be some way for me to take advantage of this roll of the number "one hundred." Then it hit me. For the next two days, I'd have my nose buried in a book, studying for a physics exam. I wasn't a great student so maybe this was my one chance to get a perfect score. Yes! That's it. I'll use the power on my test score! My first hunderd percent was in the bag!

For the next two days, I studied physics. Well, I kinda studied. Okay, I at least had the book with me while I drank cappuccinos at the A-Street Roma that evening. I had the thick textbook in my backpack on Saturday night when I met my pal Craig at The Silo for a pitcher of Coors Light. I even opened it and read a couple of test exercises as I drank coffee on my apartment balcony on Sunday.

On Monday morning, I was ready. I had never faced an exam with such confidence in my life. I sat down, the proctor handed me a test, and I jumped in. I scribbled and erased, scratched my head here and there, and wrote down answers. I wore out a couple of sheets of scratch paper, but an hour later, I handed the test back to the proctor with a smile on my face.

I had to wait until Wednesday to get my grade. But I wasn't worried. I had the power of the hunderds. Nothing could break it. If a rich senator couldn't break it, a bald-headed college professor didn't even have a chance.

On Wednesday, I walked to campus with a skip in my step. I whistled as I walked to the physics building and then climbed a few flights of stairs to the professor's office. The scores were posted on a sheet hanging outside his door. Without trepidation, I ran my finger down the sheet until it got to my student number. I closed my eyes and moved it to the right, toward the last column. With a cocky bravado, I said a loud "Bam!" and opened my eyes.

"70, C-"

Well shit. I looked around the list and there were a few that scored "100", but they certainly weren't near my name. I had gotten a lower grade than any other exam I had taken. My score had gotten worse!

The hunderd streak was broken.

Of course, it would be a few years before I could realize that coincidences happen. Sometimes they even happen several times in a row. It's no secret force of the universe or planets lining up. It's just dumb random luck. It might be fun, but it's just that. Fun. Nothing else. It'd be many more years before I could really admit that I was supposed to be studying and not using a statistical anomaly as an excuse to drink beer. I'd need a few decades of life experience before I could fully grasp that studying and commitment are what get perfect scores. Not magic. Not Accidents. Not chance or serendipity. Hard work, that's what does it. Now I'm an old man, and I'm one hunderd percent sure of it!

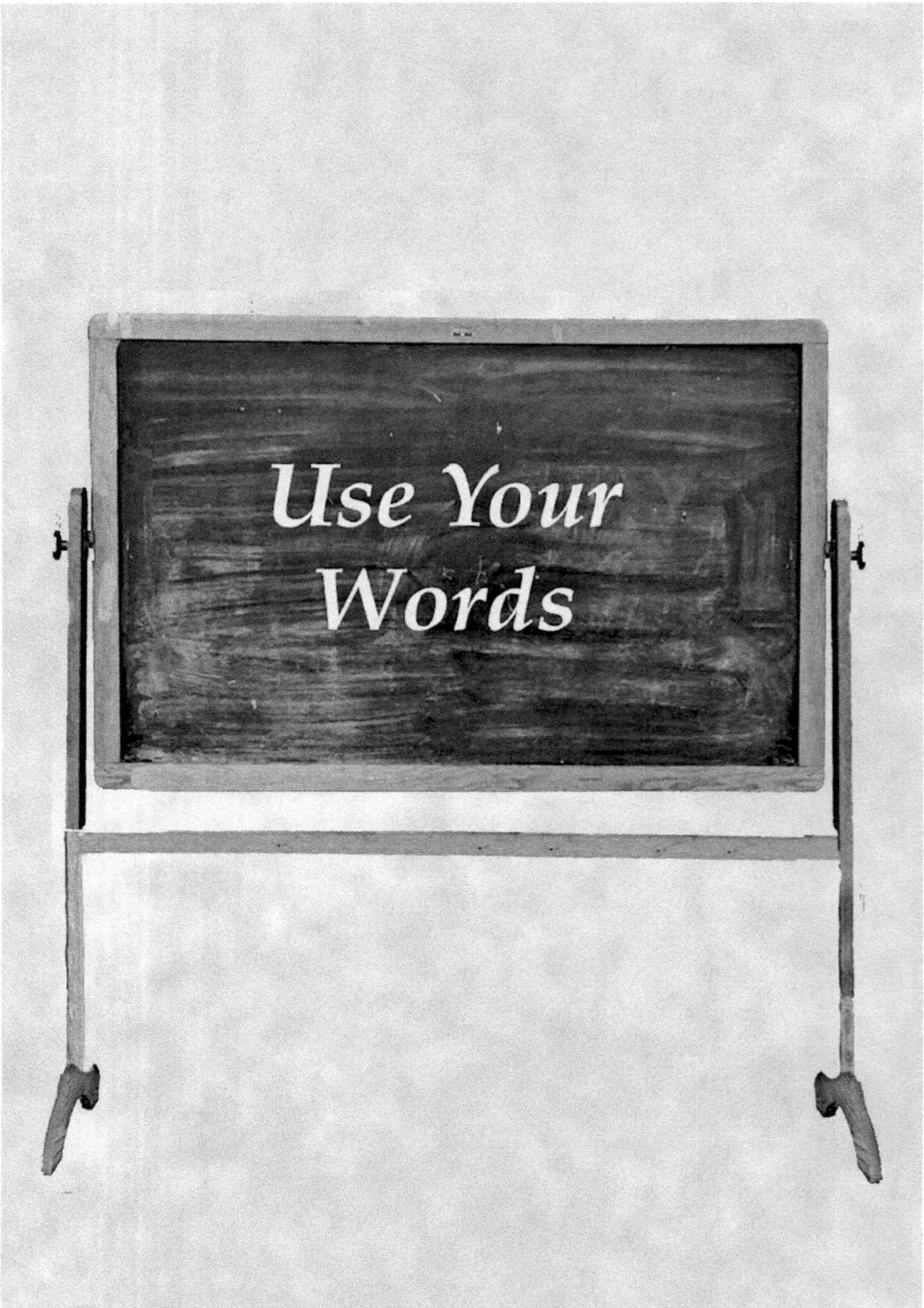
Use Your Words

29

A Teaching Moment

When I was about 25 years old and had moved from my small hometown in the San Joaquin Valley to Davis for school, I was literally "fresh off the farm." The farm was horses and tractors, work boots and leather gloves. U.C. Davis and college life was very new to me.

Within just a couple of weeks, I had met a guy named Jeff. He was nothing like me. He was a vegetarian, drove a Volkswagen bus, and wore round wire-rimmed glasses. He was from Fresno, and despite our differences, we quickly became friends.

One day, he and I were driving through Davis in my truck. An old lady was about to cross a street, so I stopped well back to give her space. The guy in a car behind me honked his horn. I glanced back at him and tried to ignore him, but within a few seconds, he honked again.

Well, that was too much for this farm boy. I threw on the emergency brake and started getting out of my truck. My friend was startled, and with a puzzled look he asked, "What the heck are you doing?"

I told him "I'll be right back. I'm gonna teach this guy a lesson!"

I jumped out of the truck and within a few big steps, I was dragging the twenty-year-old impatient driver out through his window. It was a bit of a scene, but he got his lesson.

When I got back to the truck, my peace-loving friend was appalled. In his sternest voice, he said, "You can't do stuff like that here! You can't do stuff like that anymore! It's not your job to teach people lessons!" He ended our ride by telling me that while I was in college, I might want to concentrate on being a student and leave some of my teaching duties to Karma.

He was right. So I tried and I did pretty well during my college years. But apparently in my life, I view a lot of circumstances as perfect "teaching moments."

Teaching moments naturally happen spontaneously between a child and a parent. I've seen this most often when something bad happens, and the parent sees an opportunity to make a useful lesson out of it.

My opportunities for teaching usually pop up when I encounter grown men who didn't learn valuable life lessons from their parents. They need me to teach them some stuff. On many occasions, I've taught grown men to be a lot more careful with their foul mouths in public and around my wife and kids. The adult man-students might end up with some knots on their heads and some embarrassment, but they also got a lesson.

I recall a time when I taught a valuable lesson to a pickpocket in Barcelona. I left him with one good arm so he could still try to make an *honest* living.

Those were teaching moments.

There were a lot more.

But sometimes, even the teacher becomes the student, and my personal teaching moment came about twenty years ago while I was in the middle of teaching a guy his lesson.

Anytime anyone puts hands on someone else, regardless of their "crime," you're already on shaky moral ground. But legally, you're very likely not just on shaky ground. Most likely, you'll find yourself squarely on some solid go-to-jail ground. During my particular lesson, between smacks, I looked up to see a surveillance camera looking right at me. I let the guy go and apologized. He was happy at the turn of events and made haste.

That was *my* teaching moment! And since then, I've vowed to make all my teaching moments like my momma taught me—use your words!

Now, I teach with a smile, a reasonable argument, good facts, and a solid delivery. It might be a tad less satisfying than bare knuckles from a visceral standpoint. But from a cerebral perspective, it's far more enjoyable. In fact, teaching a lesson with a strong argument ranks as one of the more satisfying things in my life.

Plus, it's nice to know that very few people end up in jail over a well-delivered verbal correction, especially when there's a smile involved.

30

What Can I Do?

I both say it and hear that a lot. I see a problem and ask, "What can I do?"

Sometimes, the problem we see is focused and local, and then it's easy to get an answer. For example, someone's house down the street burns down, and we ask, "What can I do?" Then someone responds that they are taking donated items or cash to help them replace their loss. So, we get an answer and know exactly what we can do.

Other times, it's not so easy. Some problems just seem so big that we don't even ask. Other times, there seem to be too many problems. Again, we feel helpless and don't bother to ask or think about it much.

I was thinking about this the other night. Of course, it was in the middle of the night when I should have been sleeping (yes, even I need a small amount of beauty sleep). I was thinking about a big problem that I had read about. It was big, but it probably really didn't even affect me. As I lay there in the dark, I wondered if I should even be concerned with asking myself, "What can I do?"

As I reasoned through it, I pieced together a scenario that could help me visualize it. Imagine a bunch of people living in a twenty-mile section of road. The houses towards one end are two-story, with green yards and three-car garages full of nice cars. The houses towards the other end are smaller and older, with used cars parked outside. You get the picture. Rich people on one end of the street and poorer people on the other.

Each Wednesday is garbage day. Every house rolls their garbage cans out to the street. The big garbage truck starts at the upscale end and proceeds down the street, stopping at each house. The problem arises because once the truck is full, it stops and heads to the dump, and that's it for the week.

Most weeks, the garbage truck makes its way down the entire street, and everyone gets their garbage emptied. But sometimes, when the bigger houses have a lot of garbage, the truck gets full early, and the houses towards the end of the street don't get serviced. Some of them might even miss a couple of weeks in a row.

One evening, a few of the big house neighbors were discussing the garbage problem. They had heard that some of the small house neighbors were complaining. The big house neighbors who lived early on the truck route stood around watering their green lawns and chatted. The conversation had lines like this:

"That's just the way it's always been."

"It's not just here. It's happening everywhere. It can never be fixed."

"Those people down there are always complaining about something."

"Those people down there get everything for free anyway. What are they complaining about?"

"It doesn't affect me any, so it's not my problem."

In my thought example, the two-story neighbors really highlighted the obstacles to making change happen. Each one of those thoughts gave them license to do nothing. Those kinds of comments tend to let us all off the hook without ever asking, "What can I do?"

So, I guess I answered my own question. Yes, I do need to ask, "What can I do?" I need to ask it even when the problem seems too big or even when it doesn't affect me much or at all. I need to ask it when I'm told that those people are always complaining. I certainly need to ask it when I hear that there's no solution "because it's always been that way."

But now it's time to ask a different question. Right now, I'm asking, "What can I do... to get some sleep?"

I need that beauty sleep. This beautiful face ain't gonna shine itself!

31

A Fishing Story

Any good book needs a fishing story. Sometimes a true story just falls in my lap and almost writes itself.

The sea was angry that day, my friends.

~George Costanza

The Sea of Cortez was surely angry, but beautiful. Although every day is beautiful in Cabo San Lucas. Rhonda and I had booked a fishing trip on a twenty-eight-foot boat with a captain and a deckhand. Our daughter, Teresa, was with us this time. Since we were spending her inheritance, she was insistent on getting in on some of the action before it was all gone. Unlike her brother, she had never been off-shore fishing with us. After hearing my non-stop stories about some of our recent trips, catching big marlin, sailfish, dorado, yellowtail, tuna, and other delicious fish, she was excited and ready to have her own fishing story.

A tropical storm had just passed, and an even bigger one was due any day, so we squeezed in between the storms. It was a now-or-never moment for the trip.

The sea was rough, but I can understand how people get addicted to the ocean. The sunrise was beautiful. Even with the eight-foot swells, there was both a peace and an excitement in holding the rails and rocking with the boat. Every few minutes, we'd get hit with a big wave and get drenched in spray. We could taste the salt water on our lips.

For most of the day, the fishing was pretty dead. But even then, it's always fun. The excitement of getting up early and listening for the telltale whir of a fish on a line. We know that it's called fishing and not just fish-catching. But we didn't care, it's all fun.

It was approaching the end of the day, and we hadn't even gotten a bite. But then, in an instant, one of the reels started screaming and peeling off line. We managed to get Teresa in the fighting chair and the rod into the gimble on the chair between her legs. It was a one-hundred-pound striped marlin, and the fight was on!

After ten minutes of cranking and trying to keep the one-thousand-dollar bent-over rod from disappearing into the ocean, Teresa was done. She did the exciting and hard part, but when it came down to mostly grueling work, she was ready to stand by and watch the fun. So, without too much hassle, we managed to get the fighting gear switched over to me. Fifteen minutes later, we had a squirming and writhing fish pulled into the boat for a quick photo and then back into the sea. It was quick enough that it never even dislodged the lamprey stuck to its sides.

That was the end of a long day. We were hot, tired and ready to head back to the distant shore. As we sat out in the tossing waves, Rhonda pointed to a panga bobbing in the water a short distance from us. A panga is a small skiff, more adapted to inshore fishing. It was odd to see one that far from shore, and we both wondered why it was out there. It was so small that it disappeared and then reappeared with every swell.

As we started back to the docks, the captain began yelling that he saw another marlin fin sticking out of the water near us. But before I could even locate the fin in the waves, it was on! He gunned the engines to drag the lures in the fish's direction.

I hadn't even recuperated from the previous fight, and another reel was screaming and peeling line. Teresa wasn't ready to try again, and Rhonda just went for the boat ride and scenery. So, within seconds, I was back in the hot seat.

This time, the fish had grabbed a live bait that was in the water. These are the smallest rod-and-reels on the boat. They use a much lighter leader than the other reels. To fight even a normal-sized marlin, these reels require more finesse and a lot more work by the captain to keep the boat in position and chase the fish.

I held the curved rod and watched the line disappear from the reel. As abruptly as the fish started fighting away from the boat, it switched directions and started going parallel to the boat. I raced to take up the line as the captain roared the engines to keep up with the fish.

Then we saw it! Three-hundred-fifty plus pounds of beautiful sparkling blue marlin jumping ten feet in the air! Then it jumped again. And then it jumped again and again and again. It was heart-pounding. The captain and deckhand were yelling in excitement. The captain again roared the boat at full throttle to chase the fish. The motor was loud, and my feet were planted firmly for the ride.

And then silence.

The boat's motor just died.

Silence, except for the reel's screaming drag on the rod as the fish got farther from the boat. Very quickly, it passed the boat, and we couldn't even keep the rod pointed at the fish. It was hopeless without a motor.

As I was sitting there, hopelessly watching the last of the line disappear, the little panga appeared out of nowhere. The captain yelled to their crew to come and help us. The little boat and its surprised crew came alongside us, with the boats almost bashing into each other in the angry surf. The captain motioned for me to jump in.

But I was not ready to jump into a bobbing little boat in rough seas, miles from shore! I yelled to the other captain, "Tu tomas! Tu tomas! You take it!"

With both boats hitting each other in the waves, I managed to hand off the rod to one of the fishermen in the little panga. The guy grabbed the rod, took a seat, and they roared off after the jumping fish.

I'll bring the story to its sad ending. The little boat could not keep up with the huge fish. The guy battling the rod undoubtedly had better skills than me, but he certainly had my luck. We watched in the distance as he fell backward into the little boat. The line had snapped.

Both crews were devastated. This was likely the biggest marlin on their lines in a few years. This was the size of fish that prompted the Mexican deckhand to get a marlin tattooed on his leg. They were seriously crushed. But Rhonda and I weren't. Even Teresa has adopted our "no le hacé" motto. It doesn't matter. It's all good! Who cares?

The captain spent a little while working on the boat but finally gave up. It wasn't a field repair. The tiny little panga crew threw us a rope and towed us for several miles back to shore. With no motor, very little shade, and traveling at about one mile per hour, it was painfully hot. The boat tossed like a champagne cork in a storm for the two-hour tow back to the marina.

It was brutal at the time, but that was then. Today, it's a wonderful memory and a story for the grandkids.

The big marlin is still out there and getting even bigger.

It's got my name on it.

I'll be back.

32

Nashville Style

Around our house, when it comes to hot wings, Rhonda doesn't mess around. For ten years, we hosted an annual horseshoe tournament and hot wing contest, so we've tasted some good ones! At our parties, we had custom t-shirts for everybody, big silver trophy buckles for the horseshoe winners, and a gold chicken trophy for the best hot wings. We also tried to round out the fun by helping a local children's home. Leading up to our tenth and final year in 2006, with the help of our friends, we raised much-needed awareness and almost $10,000 for a local adoption service.

I think most came for the horseshoes, but some only came to win that prized hot wing trophy. Most everyone put in their best effort and even came adorning signs to help market their gourmet creations.

My hot wing recipe was called Double Trouble. I never won anything, but they were hot! They were hot when you ate them and then they were extra hot the next day. Double Trouble.

Rhonda always put more effort into it and went for the perfect balance between heat and flavor. Just recently, I watched her make another batch. Here is what I saw.

First, soak the wings in a bath of buttermilk, hot sauce, pickle juice, and one beaten egg. Let them soak for as long as you can let them sit. When you can't stand it anymore, go to the next step.

Coat the wet wings with a mixture of flour and seasonings, like garlic, onion, paprika, black and cayenne pepper, and baking powder, or whatever you think is perfect. No measuring. A dash of this and a hint of that.

Then, deep fry them in peanut oil (or Crisco). When that's done, they're delicious fried chicken—but they're not hot wings just yet.

Here's where you change them from spicy fried chicken to richly flavored hot wings. Brush on a coating of sauce made from a mixture of a little bit of the frying oil, hot sauce, honey, garlic powder, salt, and again, whatever you see fit.

Serve with your favorite side, and you're set. We had corn on the cob.

Like we say around here, "It sho' am good!"

33

Reboot My Heart

Some things never change. Or, perhaps better stated, old problems are still problems.

I'm probably as high-tech as any old man can be. My smartphone is never more than a year old. It gives me messages, takes pictures, and tells me where to turn to get where I want to go. My smart watch tells me how far I've walked, how fast my heart beats, how much time I spend in REM sleep, and even talks to my phone. My thermostat looks around the house to see if anyone needs some AC or Heat. Our washer and dryer sends us a message when the clothes are ready. Even our refrigerator thinks for us. I Tweet, IG, Tic-Tok and Facebook. There's more, but you get the point.

Yet, despite the high-tech bubble around me, there are some old problems that still haven't been solved.

A guy I recently met was asking me questions about the time a few years ago when I was deathly sick. He asked some specific questions about my time on the ventilator. I was in a coma and don't remember anything other than some high-tech equipment was saving my life. He asked me if I was ever scared. I responded, "Hell yeah I was scared! I thought I was gonna die almost every day!" He asked when I was the scaredest? So, I told him the story of when my heart started beating three hundred beats per minute, and I thought it was gonna explode.

The hospital was loud, even at night. Sleep was difficult, but one morning

I was startled awake from a deep sleep. There were no beeps or alarms, but I could feel my heart racing and genuinely going crazy. I was connected to dozens of wires on my chest that all led up to an array of digital machines. They blinked and beeped and kept perfect track of every aspect of my body. If anything went out of line, an alarm would sound, and someone would come quickly to check on me.

But when my heart went crazy, no one came running in. I pushed the red button to call the nurse, but still no one came in. So I pushed it again. And again. And again.

Soon, a nurse peeked in and asked if I needed something. Wide-eyed, I told her my heart was going crazy. She walked in and looked up at the instruments for a few seconds. She took out her stethoscope, placed it in her ears, and then put the cold round disc on my chest. Instantly, her eyes widened. She glanced back up at the displays, undoubtedly wondering why there weren't alarms and buzzers screaming for attention.

This is where I realized that all of the high-tech in the world might still have some old-fashioned problems. I was a bit disgusted when she reached down on my chest and started wiggling wires like she was reaching under the hood of an old truck! She wiggled a couple, then a couple more. Then all hell broke loose! She found it! A bad connection!

This would have been bad enough, but it gets worse. The room filled up with people pretty quickly. In haste, they shaved my chest and added new wires and electrodes. A doctor came in and tried a few things. Nothing worked. My heart was still pounding away, and I was scared to death. The doc gave some directions to a couple of the nurses and then started talking to me.

"Mr Jones, I'm going to inject you with a drug that will stop your heart for ten seconds. When it restarts, it should start back at a normal pace. Do you understand?"

I told him, "Yes, I understand." But I went further, though, to loudly express my dissatisfaction that I'm surrounded by a million dollars worth of high-tech equipment, and the best thing he could come up with to fix my heart was to turn it off, then turn it back on, and see what happens.

What the heck? Rebooting is for computers, not living hearts!

Well, low-tech saved me. I'm here. They wiggled wires and then rebooted my heart.

But that's all I can write for today. My thousand-dollar phone is beeping about a low battery. I've got to yank the charger cable out and blow in the hole a few times, wiggle it, and try again. Low-tech. That'll fix it!

34

The Mexican

I love being in airport lounges and meeting people from all over our
country and the world. As much as our country intermingles, the
various parts of it have still managed to keep the most important part
of their unique identities—their accents. Two sentences in, you can tell when
someone's from Boston or Wisconsin. Anyone can spot the beautiful sweet
tea drawl of the Deep South or the French influence in Louisiana. Even if
you've never watched a single episode of Fargo, the mid-western accent is
hard to miss. And don't even get me started on our Canadian neighbors to
the north. I love the variety of accents and dialects, and that diversity just
deepens what I love about America.

I've been told that the same dialects and accents can also be found among
Mexico's thirty-two states. Native Spanish speakers can tell if someone is
from Sonora or Chihuahua in the north or Oaxaca and Tabasco in the south.
There are differences between the seaside states of Yucatan and Veracruz
and the mountainous states of Zacatecas and Guanajuato. I'm sure it's true,
but it's all just Spanish to me.

I learned both English and Spanish in the San Joaquin Valley in California.
For the next fifty years, I fine-tuned my English. I learned and unlearned
words. In my thirty-plus years as a biologist, I've undoubtedly written over
a million words. A fraction of it was popular writing, but the bulk of it was
boring scientific writing. Boring or not, it still needed to be written correctly.

I learned it. I studied it. I took criticism, but I finally got good at it.

On the other hand, my Spanish has had very little growth. But as bad as it is, I love to use it. Rhonda and I spend at least a month each year in Mexico. And Mexicans are very gracious with my bad Spanish. They laugh with me and help me along. Several of them love to joke that I gain a few more words with every Corona. A six-pack in, and I'm talking Spanish with everyone around us. I try to speak only Spanish when I'm in Mexico, and it gets better with every trip.

Mexico isn't the only country that uses Spanish. Many countries in Central and South America speak Spanish. Even Spain in Europe's Iberian Peninsula uses Spanish, hence the name! But that's where the dialects and accents enter the picture. Spanish in Spain is not the same Spanish as in Mexico. My choppy San Joaquin Valley Spanish in Spain couldn't even order me a cup of coffee correctly. It's probably like the difference between American English and British or Irish English. I've watched movies where the Irish English needed subtitles. My Spanish in Spain needed subtitles.

But still, I'm not deterred. I try to use it at any opportunity. Rhonda is even trying, as well. She had no opportunity to learn Spanish growing up in Alabama, so she has much catching up to do. We try to speak Spanish at home, or at least we use Spanglish. She has come a long way, but it is daunting.

A couple of years ago, we were sitting in lounge chairs by a small pool at a hotel in Cabo San Jose, at the southern tip of Baja California. The hotel had a small outdoor restaurant and bar located a short distance from the pool. The lone waiter and bartender spoke no English. We sat in our lounge chairs and drank a Corona, the unofficial gringo beer of Mexico. It was hot out, so we decided to have one more and an order of nachos. As I got up to go order, in a bold move, Rhonda insisted that I let her handle it. I reminded her that none of the staff spoke any English. But she was undaunted. She would do it.

I had her rehearse for me before she left.

Nosotros quedemos dos mas Coronas y un plato de nachos con pollo. Por favor.

It sounded pretty good to me, and off she went. I watched the waiter greet her at the edge of the shade, and she started talking. She said some words and held up two fingers. The waiter said some words back, and Rhonda nodded. He said a few more words and pointed his finger in my direction. Rhonda nodded and left.

"Well, how did it go"

"I don't know. It seemed pretty straightforward, but then he started saying a whole rapid-fire string of Spanish, so I just nodded."

We both knew that nodding is dangerous.

"Well, ya vermos. We'll see. I'm sure he got it just fine, Baby."

We both watched in anticipation. Looking through the open restaurant, we could mostly only see silhouettes, but the waiter was walking around and even made a trip to speak to the bartender. In a few minutes, he headed our way. But he had no bottles and no plate in his hand. He walked up to us and handed me our bill. I looked at Rhonda and chuckled. I added a tip and signed my name.

He said, "Muchas gracias," and headed back to the restaurant.

Once he was out of earshot, we busted up laughing. Somehow Rhonda's simple "dos mas, por favor" had turned into "La quinta, por favor."

Rhonda stopped laughing and looked me in the eyes. "That's it. I'm done!"

I went and got us a couple of beers and came back to convince Rhonda to keep trying. I assured her that it would make a great story someday.

A few months ago, Rhonda and I were in Bocas Del Toro, an island in Panama. We were on a rattly boat dock behind a little grocery store. We were supposed to get picked up by a guy named Brown in his little boat. As he puttered up in the boat, we waved and pointed towards our luggage and bags of groceries. He killed the noisy engine, and I started speaking Spanish, letting him know that we were happy to see him. Before I even finished my sentences, he let out a big laugh and said in a loud voice, "The Mexican! You're a Mexican!"

I tried to explain to him that I was actually from California but to no avail. To him, I was "the Mexican." Once we got to the little dock at our hut and tossed out the bags, he didn't stick around long enough for me to have a couple of cold Panama beers and see if my Spanish got any more Panamanian.

For the next week, every time he motored past our hut, he stood up in his boat, cupped his hand around his mouth, and yelled, "the Mexican!" Then he'd laugh and wave. I'd laugh and wave back.

The Mexican. I was proud of it. I had a Mexican accent.

I've always said that you can call me anything. Just don't call me late for dinner!

35

Odds Are

Almost everything in a kid's life seems to have some kind of near-calculable risk associated with it. Most everything we did had something that you could bet on or against. Yes or no. Will or won't. Success or failure. Caught or skated by.

My brother Steve riding his new Honda Elsinore 250 motorcycle at break-neck speeds down our dirt roads.

Odds are: If he doesn't slow that thing down, he's gonna end up with a broken neck.

My cousin Bruce taking a running start to jump over an irrigation ditch full of water.

Odds are: He's gonna have two feet full of mud!

My cousin Mitch, climbing onto a wild horse's back.

Odds are: He's gonna end up flat on his ass.

It was a hot summer morning, but there was no school. We weren't quite old enough for Dad to put us to hard labor. Steve and I sat on buckets in the shade beside our barn. It was always a good place to sit. The little private spot was on the opposite side of our house, so we were well out of Mom's view through the kitchen window. We could see up the only two roads leading to our place and could always tell if anyone was coming our way.

As was often the case on fresh summer mornings, we were between shenanigans. Our mornings sometimes took a while to get rolling. Sometimes, there just didn't seem to be much to do. When we were bored, we'd sit around and complain to each other. It didn't matter that we were in the middle of a two-thousand-acre playground with animals, trees, bicycles, and other kids, just a short fifteen-minute walk away. Sometimes, the gamut of opportunities just played out.

We were each drinking a Coke from the little green bottles that you now only see in old movies. Steve took his last drink and then sat with the empty bottle in his hand. Bottles were precious. You could return them to the store and get a nickel.

Steve stood up and looked around. There was some odds-and-ends lumber stacked against the barn. He eyed the scattered pieces of four-by-four rounded fence posts and random cut-off pieces of plywood. Steve's brain worked in mysterious ways. The assorted lumber went through his mind on one side and came out the other side with an idea. Let's build a catapult!

Without even telling me his idea, he rolled one of the long round fence posts over to the hidden side of the barn. He then grabbed a six-foot-long piece of a two-by-four board and laid it across so it sat like a little see-saw. He carefully put his Coke bottle on the lower end and looked it over. The upper end of the see-saw was about a foot off the ground. He looked at me, jumped up, and stomped the board as hard as his fifty-pound body could stomp.

The Coke bottle shot up about twenty feet into the air in a close arc, then fell back into the dirt with a thud. The Coke bottle catapult was born.

We both got excited and tried it again. This time, we dragged a bale of straw next to it so that I, with my heavier body, could jump off and hit the catapult with more force. It worked, and the bottle went even higher and further, making a whirring sound before it landed back on the ground.

We launched the bottle a bunch of times, trying different methods to make it go higher. We didn't know anything about fulcrums, or levers, or forces, but with most every reconfiguration, we managed to send the bottle higher and higher.

Odds are: They're gonna break something and get their asses whipped.

When it seemed that we had tried everything possible with a piece of lumber, a fence post, a Coke bottle, and a human body for mass, Steve's brain gave it one more try. "What if we move everything closer to the barn and use a rope to drag another fence post up on top? We could drop it off the barn straight down to the catapult."

He didn't have to tell me twice.

Scaling the barn wasn't an issue. We spent a lot of time on that roof. It was a perfect lookout to survey our surroundings and was the spot every farm kid had spent at night, lying back and trying to count the stars. But getting a one-hundred-pound fence post up there might be a challenge.

We easily managed to find a couple of pieces of rope lying around the barn. We tied them to the fence post and threw the ends over the roof. With both of us at the roof peak, we were surprised at how easily the smooth round post dragged up the sloped roof. Steve would pull and then hold. Then I would pull and hold. In less than five minutes, the post was sitting on top, balanced across the roof's peak.

We rolled the heavy post over towards the edge of the roof. Steve held it while I climbed down to set up the catapult. It had to be perfect. The end of the raised board had to be exactly below the end of the roof. I got everything in place.

"Hurry, Rawge, I can't hardly hold this anymore!"

"Just hold it! Don't drop it!"

I grabbed a little dirt clod and made my way back up. As I helped Steve steady the cumbersome fence post, I dropped the little piece of dirt from the roof peak. It was the last test. The tiny dirt rock hit the top of the fulcrum in the perfect spot. The Coke bottle catapult was ready. It was launch time.

"Okay, Steve. We'll roll it to the edge, make sure it's exactly level, and then roll it off. It has to stay flat. Got it?"

Steve nodded, and we carefully rolled the round log to the edge.

I counted off, "Three-Two-One-Go!"

I watched the post roll over the edge. I could tell it was perfect. In an instant, the loud whirring bottle went flying past our heads. But this time, the whirring sound was louder. This time everything was different. This time the bottle didn't head in the direction of the open pasture. Nope. This time the bottle was headed in the direction of our house.

Our yard, house, driveway, barn, and pasture all sat on about two acres, surrounded by thousands of acres of farmland. Two acres is 87,120 square feet. Our house was 1200 square feet. Mom's car was about 130 square feet. The math says that about 85,700 square feet were available for a safe landing.

Odds are...

We watched the green bottle travel higher and higher, well past our expectations. My little brain watched the bottle's arc and was rapidly doing mental calculations, like a NASA computer trying to pinpoint Apollo-11's re-entry into the Pacific Ocean. As every split-second piece of data entered my mind, it re-calculated the landing spot. Halfway through the descent, I had it locked in. The green bottle would land exactly on the roof of Mom's car!

At that point, all we could do was watch and brace ourselves. We knew nothing about objects falling from the sky, and thanks to good ol' dependable gravity, they accelerated at 9.8 m/s/s (meters per second squared). We knew none of that math. But even a dumb farm kid could tell that the bottle was falling fast. The bottle wouldn't touch down with a dull thud like our previous launches. This was going to be a dramatic landing.

We watched the tumbling bottle until the last moment, and then we braced for impact. In less than a heartbeat, the bottle shattered into a million pieces... on the concrete, less than a foot from mom's precious red car.

We looked at each other with wide *"OH SHIT"* eyes. I looked up the road. It was ten o'clock. We quickly started calculating our odds.

Dad wouldn't be home for lunch for at least an hour.

Odds are: He'll never find out.

I could see all the way into the kitchen through the window, just across from mom's car.

Odds are: Mom was in the living room reading her book and not yet in the kitchen, making lunch.

The windows were all closed but the crashing bottle was so loud.

Odds are: She wouldn't have heard it, especially if the swamp cooler was whirring away down the hall.

We watched for a minute. And then another. No truck came roaring down the road, and no angry face came to peer at the window. No doors flung open, and no voice yelled out, "What the hell have you two boys done now?"

Odds are: We could skate by.

Without a word or a plan, we skidded down the tar paper roof and shimmied down the wooden orchard ladder propped against the side. We ran towards the house but split paths at the driveway. I ran for the push broom and big dust-pan while Steve looked for a cardboard box.

As I feverishly pushed and pulled the broom, Steve held the dustpan and dumped the dirt and glass into the box. We both instinctively knew that if we could sweep up every tiny speck of glass, we could dodge a bullet.

We swept frantically in every direction from one end of the driveway to the other. Dad had poured the concrete so that Mom could park her car on something solid. She might need to drive down a muddy road to get there, but she could park and walk up to the house without getting her feet muddy. The driveway was the only piece of concrete on the whole property and Dad was proud of it.

Before long, we had the whole driveway near spotless and were lying down, trying to reach the broom beneath the car and get the last of the shiny shards. But as I reached the broom across the concrete, I heard a rumbling noise behind me. I turned to see Dad's blue Chevy truck pull up to the house.

Steve and I both stood up and feigned a smile.

"Look at you boys! Dang! That looks nice! Thank you!"

Our feigned smiles turned into genuine smiles. He was proud of us.

"Just trying to do our parts," I said with a cocky grin.

"Let me go get your mom's keys and I'll back it up so you can get underneath."

The happy grin disappeared. I knew there was one hundred and thirty square feet of bright and sparkly glass hidden beneath the red fenders.

Before I could say anything. Steve's amazing brain kicked in.

"That's okay, Dad. We like crawling under there. It's like a game to us. It's fun!" he said in a believable voice.

Dad stood for a minute.

"Okay. Well, finish it and clean up. Let's eat lunch."

We scrambled and the stiff broom pulled the last of the glass from beneath the car. We dumped the box of glass into the big trash can near the barn. We washed our hands and faces in the outside sink. Just before we opened the back door, Steve had a suggestion.

"We could try it again, but with a parachute!"

I gave him a disgusted look. We had just miraculously dodged an ass-whooping. If I knew anything, I occasionally knew to quit while you're ahead. This was one of those "just walk away" moments

Dad bragged about us at lunch. We beat the odds.

I was nine years old. Today I'm sixty-four. "Odds are" seems to have been built into my life. Even with years of practice, I never got very good at the calculations. I occasionally won, but like any other gamble, I've lost more than I've won.

Fifteen years old.

Odds are... It's heavy enough. It doesn't even need to be tied down.

Sixteen years old.

Odds are... There's not a sheriff between here and town. Let's see how fast this thing can go!

Seventeen years old.

Odds are... The math test will be just like the practice test. I don't even need to

study.

Eighteen years old.

Odds are... He won't see the first swing coming.

The rest of my life.

Odds are... It'll never happen to me.

36

Dreams

Man, I had a weird dream the other night. Most of my dreams are just a stupid rambling hodge-podge of everything I've encountered or thought about in the past day or so. This one was different. This one was perfect.

Rhonda and I were in a rustic cabin somewhere in the mountains. I walked outside and found two beautiful quarter horses tied to a rail, standing patiently with their Billy Cook saddles and silver gilded bridles.

The horses were beautiful and perfectly muscled. The saddles and bridles were the kind of western equipment I'd dreamed of as a kid. I've never even sat in a saddle that nice.

Looking down a trail, about a dozen other cabins had two or three horses tied in front. Somehow, in the dream, I knew that we were there to work some cattle with the other cowboys. Again, this is a dream situation. I've worked cows before, but never in such perfect surroundings.

As Rhonda stood outside, patting the horses' necks, a couple of non-cowboy characters dressed in nice suits and ties walked up. They introduced themselves as the lawyer and public information officer for the cattle outfit. They started talking business.

The well-dressed pair told us that within a day, one person at the ranch was going to die. They apologized, but they said that they didn't know which one of the working folks it was going to be. They continued and told us that they also didn't know if it was due to the food, the water, or just something in the air.

I was startled and a bit panicked, remembering, even in my dream, that just four years earlier, I had spent a few weeks living at death's door. I don't want to die. I looked at Rhonda with fear in my eyes.

Rhonda is wonderful. She's calming and reassuring. She's also a previous high school mathlete. She loves math. In her calm voice, she started in with some math to try to make me feel better. She said there were about twenty people in the camp, so at worst, one of us had about a one in twenty chance of being the dead person. She did some more math and said that if we didn't eat or drink any water and remove those from the probability, our chances of death went way down.

I instantly felt better. We'd make sure to take advantage of every mitigating factor. With no food and no drinks, we would move well into the "not gonna happen to us" territory.

Just as I calmed down, the camp cookie walked up the trail carrying a couple of big steaming plates of dripping sweet BBQ ribs and a jar of cold homemade lemonade.

I looked at it for less than a second and immediately turned to Rhonda, "I'm taking my chances," and I reached for the plate!

I'm sure there's a moral in there somewhere. Maybe it's that we are often our own worst enemies. Or perhaps it's a warning about the dangers of giving in to our own desires.

But that's not why I'm telling this true story. I'm putting it out here because I want people to know that if I ever disappear, it's because I got lured into a creepy white van with BBQ ribs.

Look for those guys!

37

Fight or Flight

Over half my life, I was afraid to travel. For years, I lived less than two hours from San Fransisco and had never even seen the beautiful city. I had only ever flown one time on a commercial flight. I had flown from Fresno to Las Vegas to fish in a championship bass tournament. I was the only person on the forty-person propeller plane who wasn't WWF. I sat in awe in the back row as I watched Hulk Hogan, Randy "Macho Man" Savage, Hill-Billy Jim, and all the other characters pile into the plane. They had finished a show in Fresno's Selland Arena and were headed to Vegas.

The plane had one seat on one side and two seats on the other. For the next two hours, I sat nervously, trying to avoid any conversation with my across-the-aisle seatmate, Miss Elizabeth. She chatted at me while Macho Man slept against the window. I just wanted to be left alone. I had seen what Macho Man did to any wrestler who flirted with his girlfriend. But she wanted to talk about bass fishing.

When the plane landed, Elizabeth offered to leave me a ticket at will-call. I thanked her but politely declined.

My fight-or-flight instinct kicked in and told me, "Flight!" I didn't want no trouble!

Years later, Rhonda coaxed me into accompanying her to San Francisco for some business workshops and a Christmas party. We would stay at the Sir Frances Drake Hotel. We arrived in Rhonda's car and were greeted by a valet attendant and doorman wearing beefeater royal guard costumes. I was stunned just walking into the beautiful lobby. The forty-foot ceiling was gilded with beautiful architectural elements.

We were staying on the top floor, and our room had a magnificent view of the city. I was mesmerized. I stood at the corner window and stared at the huge city, something that I had never seen. I chuckled at myself when, fifteen minutes later, I realized that the only other people that I could see gazing from their own hotel windows were children. I was as enchanted as an eight-year-old kid.

The next day, while Rhonda was in meetings and workshops, I grabbed my Nikon camera and headed out to explore the city. I walked for blocks, looking up at the buildings and taking pictures of anything that caught my eye. It was all beautiful. I walked for over two hours.

But somewhere in the walk, I'd lost my way. Suddenly, it wasn't beautiful anymore. The gorgeous buildings were gone. And suddenly, I wasn't the only one doing all of the looking. The sidewalks and building steps were full of shady characters and they all seemed to be looking at me and my expensive camera. The more I walked, the worse it got. Before long, I realized I was lost, and three men were following just a few steps behind.

My fight-or-flight reflex again said, "Flight!"

As I hustled down the sidewalk towards... well, back towards where I thought I had come from... I spotted a yellow taxi coming my way. I'd never ridden in a taxi before, but I'd seen enough TV shows to know how it works. I stepped out into the street and waved my hand. I let out a breath of relief when it pulled next to me and stopped. I opened up the door and slid in.

"Where to?" the driver asked in the voice he'd undoubtedly asked a million times.

"Brother, I don't even know. I can't remember the name of the hotel. But everyone there wears some kind of fancy costumes."

"The Sir Francis Drake?"

"Yes! That's it! Thank you!"

The driver pulled back onto the street and started driving.

"What's the name of this neighborhood?" I asked.

"This is the Tenderloin. It's not exactly the best part of the city. What are you doing down here?"

"This is my first time in San Fransisco. I was just out walking."

"Well, you ventured out of the tourist's path, for sure."

In a few minutes, he pulled up to the costumed Beefeater at the entrance to the hotel. He opened my door. I paid the driver and stepped out. Before the door closed, he yelled out to me,

"Get a map, cowboy!"

I certainly would. I don't want no trouble.

The San Fransisco trip changed me. Rhonda and I dressed up and went to the extravagant party. We sat on a rooftop and drank mojitos with the other guests. I looked out over the city's beautiful nightscape. I was hooked. I wanted to see more.

New York was next. Then Seattle, New Orleans, La Jolla, Lake Tahoe, Balboa Island, and other cities followed. I still wanted more. Rhonda was adventurous and booked us a trip to Cabo San Lucas, Mexico. Then other Mexico cities followed. Then other countries. Spain, France and Italy. Then central American countries like Panama, Honduras, and Belize. Then, we visited the Caribbean and the Bahamas. You've got the idea. We've worn out some luggage.

With Rhonda's help, I overcame my travel fears. I know there will always be problems. That's just the nature of travel. Delayed flights and missed connections. Lost luggage. Miserable overnights in an uncomfortable airport chair. Taxi rides over bumpy streets. It's all going to happen.

I'm not afraid. I don't fear people in foreign countries. I'm not afraid of language barriers or the often dimly-lit streets. I don't bristle at the sound of a siren or even flinch at a hollered word. I don't fear much when it comes to travel.

Well, not much outside the Bocas Del Toro airport.

The big airport in Panama City is a breeze. You deplane, navigate your way to baggage claims, and grab your stuff. You drag your bags through customs and hand them your form and passports. Then you're on your way. The smaller airport, a half-hour taxi ride from the larger airport, is not much different. It's just a lot smaller and with a much bigger language barrier. But my limited Spanish gets us by. It's not a problem.

It's the little jungle airport once we land in Bocas that scares me. It scares me the most on the return trip. It's a small airport with only a single terminal. When you enter, everyone in the place is dressed in military fatigues, black jungle boots, and carrying a machine gun. All of them.

The agents at the security checkpoint wear the same outfits, complete with machine guns. As you pass through the baggage screen, there are two or three more machine-gun-toting men, each standing with a German Shepherd tugging at their leashes. It's all quite intimidating.

Once you're through the security, you enter a small waiting room. Inside, there are about forty chairs and a long window facing the little gravel and asphalt tarmac. The room has no air conditioning and is always as hot as Hades. The Bocas prop plane holds sixty people, so twenty people will be standing in the waiting room if the plane is full. But we all stand when the dogs arrive.

Before boarding, they line up every piece of luggage, bag, surfboard, and guitar case, side by side, outside in front of the long window. When it's ready, one of the machine-gun-toting dog handlers leads the sniffing canine down the row of bags. Everyone watches. It's nerve-wracking. I know what's in my bags. Nothing but dirty clothes. I don't have drugs or guns. I have absolutely nothing to worry about. Or do I?

That's when the fear sets in. What if my bag rubbed against another bag that does have drugs in it? What if someone slipped something into my bag? It's not locked. What if they wanted to frame me so they could demand the $87 in cash Rhonda has in her wallet? What if...

Oh phew! They're past my bag. I can unclench! I'm safe.

Once, after the dogs finished and everyone sat back down for the wait, Rhonda and I, as well as everyone else in the cramped room, turned back to small talk. We had about half an hour before boarding. A couple of hot minutes later, one of the soldiers entered the room with his machine gun across his chest. He looked the room over and then headed straight for me.

"Roger Jones?" he said, looking me straight in the eyes.

"Yes, sir." I trembled.

"Come with me."

I glanced at Rhonda. She had the same fear on her face that I was sure I had on mine. I stood up, and the security guard motioned with the barrel of his gun for me to walk ahead of him. As I walked the forty or so steps to the door, I glanced around at the other waiting passengers. The few who could bear to look at me were wide-eyed and wondering what I had done.

My fight-or-flight response again said, "Flight!" But my flight wasn't ready to board. I had no means to "flight!"

I walked slowly and stepped through the door into the security and baggage screening area. As I rounded the corner, there was a chorus of laughter. I looked up to see my friend, Jorge, still wearing the cowboy hat I had given him just two days earlier, laughing hysterically.

"I got you, Señor Rawge!" he yelled through a big grin.

He and I had talked a lot during the preceding couple of weeks. I had told him about my apprehensions at the airport including that all the guns and dogs made me nervous. He played soccer with the security men. They all got a good laugh out of it.

I didn't. My fight or flight was still screaming "flight," and I didn't calm down until we were in the air!

The fight-or-flight reflex is real. Mine rarely says fight. I'll take a flight to Barcelona or a flight of sparkling wine anytime. It's all about survival. And God knows... I don't want no trouble!

Obituary

He was a great man

Ranoje Jones, 51
of Sacramento Calif

38

You're Dead to Me

We've all heard it said or maybe even said it to someone. "You're dead to me!" After today, I might start treating everyone like they're dead to me. Sound crazy? Well, maybe not.

I was going through some junk, and I found an obituary of a not-so-close friend who died a few decades ago. We weren't close and I really didn't care much for the guy. I thought he was mildly lazy, probably not a good husband, didn't take good care of his house and property, and generally didn't measure up to my standards for a man. If anyone had asked me about him back then, I wouldn't have given a good report and treated him as such.

When I started reading through his obituary (you know, where people only say nice things about people), I was amazed at what I saw. I read about all his volunteer efforts and his life-long struggle with a disease that often kept him from work. There were beautiful quotes from his wife and kids. I learned of his work in the Peace Corps well before I knew him. There was more, but my point is this—there was a lot of good in him that I missed. I missed it until he was dead, and people went out of their way to see and share the good.

So, I'm making a commitment to try to look at people through the obituary mentality. I'm ready to look harder to see the good. I'll concentrate on their best but do it while they're alive. I'll think obituary, but I won't wait for the bad news.

From now on, you're all dead to me!

39

Ready to Fight

I haven't been in a fight in a long time because I've mastered the art of intimidation. If someone gives me a hard stare, I just throw my hands up, open my eyes way up and start acting crazy. As loudly as I can, I start yelling.

"You want some of this?"

"Come on, punk. I'll put a knot on your head so big it'll get snow on it!"

"One more step and I'll turn you into the tooth fairy's best customer."

"Listen, tough guy, I'll throw so many blows at you so fast that you'll be yelling, 'all of you need to get off me!'"

So that's how I avoid the fight. I holler out lots of crazy stuff like that, and it works pretty well!

Okay, I'm just being funny. I'm committed to being a lover, not a fighter, for the rest of my life. But just in case, I'll keep a handful of crazy lines tucked away in my back pocket.

"Listen here, son! If you ever see me fightin' a bear, then you better jump in and help...

...the bear!"

40

Memory Seeds

Throughout our lives, we constantly change. We turn directions, we age, we move in and out of interests, we meet people and lose people. It's a process, and we're all different.

But in one respect, we're all the same. Someday, we will all turn into memories. We will be gone from this Earth and will remain only in the memories of our friends and family.

We will be memories in photographs. We will be the warm thoughts when someone sees a gift we gave them or a trinket we made for them. Someday, we will be the smile on someone's face because they found a card or a note that we wrote. Someday, we will all be those things. It is sure.

But that's someday. Today is when we write those memories. Today is when we leave the little traces that will someday become smiles. Today is when we plant the seeds that will be flowers in someone's mind when we are gone.

Let us not get so busy that we forget to tend our gardens.

41

Angels Among Us

T he Bible talks plenty about angels, and we all have a vision of them. They are mostly women with long flowing dresses and beautiful white wings that can carry them about. We tell ourselves that angels are unseen but follow us around, watching over us and keeping calamity at bay.

I like all of that, but I think it's more Hollywood than King James. Even if I don't understand all of the details, the Bible still hints that they are around.

Throughout my life, I've hopped through different passions and interests. I've made wind chimes. I've built motorcycles. I've done woodworking. About twenty-five years ago, I started polishing rocks.

For a year or so, producing beautiful wet-looking, shiny rocks was my passion. I collected them everywhere and often brought them home in buckets. I bought a little tumbler that produced a small handful of beautiful smooth stones every month. And then I bought a bigger one. And then a bigger one. And then I built my own that could polish a hundred pounds of rough rocks at a time. I was obsessed. I wanted prettier rocks. I wanted greens and purples. I wanted ambers and pinks. I wanted jade.

During the height of my rock-loving phase, I accompanied Rhonda on one of her business trips to San Fransisco. We stayed in a hotel downtown. Rhonda would visit clients all day while I was free just to bum around the City.

One morning, I bought a coffee from a sidewalk vendor and found the perfect spot to sit down and people-watch in Union Square. The little park had a series of concrete steps leading from the sidewalk up to the park, which sat above the street. The long concrete steps were also long benches, perfect for sitting. I sat at the bustling corner of Geary and Powell Streets, watching the hundreds of people who crossed the street with every green light.

The street was full of tourists carrying cameras and maps. I watched as they crossed the busy street, unfolded their maps, and then pointed towards something ahead. Just behind the tourists, were the business folks. They wore suits and carried briefcases. Scattered in were some locals, out walking their little dogs or carrying bags, as they shopped.

Sprinkled in with all the "good" folks were the occasional homeless people. They carried their overstuffed plastic bags, undoubtedly filled with everything they owned. They meandered about, looking for a handout or, like me, just looking for a safe place to sit down.

As I sat on my bench, content to watch the never-ending throng of people, someone caught my eye. A lady pushed her way through the people gathered on the sidewalk, waiting for the light to change. Her head was bent down and she hustled like she was on a mission. She pushed her way to the front of the crowd and then stepped into the crosswalk, against the red flashing hand that blatantly signaled, "Do not cross!"

I lightly gasped as she continued across the street. With her head still down, she weaseled between moving cars and made her way safely to the other side. When she found the sidewalk, she didn't pause, she turned a sharp right and marched directly in my direction. In amazement, I watched her march up the concrete steps until she had reached my row, turn and then walk straight towards me. I was the only person on the steps. When she reached me, she pivoted and plopped down as close as possible, beside me.

Before I could say a word, she lifted her head up and exclaimed, "I know you love rocks, and I want to show you something!"

Again, before I could respond, she reached into her tattered purse and pulled out a little black velvet bag with a thin drawstring holding the contents safely inside. I watched as she tugged at the bag's opening, and poured out a dozen or so beautiful little gems into her hand. Each was about the size of a marble.

She looked at them for a moment, picked up the green one, and then turned to me. "I'm going to sell the others, but I want you to have this one."

I was a bit shocked, I looked closely at the lady's face. Surely, I must know her. How would she possibly know of my fascination with rocks? As I looked her over, I responded, "No, ma'am, I couldn't take that. It's too precious."

"Oh, I insist!" she responded with some authority. With that, she placed the green stone into my hand.

"Well, thank you. I promise I'll cherish it."

The lady looked at me, nodded her head, and smiled. "You're welcome. Have a nice day."

As quickly as she sat down, the little lady stood back up and, again in a hustle, headed back the way she came. She walked back down the concrete steps, turned again, and disappeared into the Geary Street crowd.

I shook my head. What the heck just happened?

The lady was about sixty years old. She wasn't wearing a white flowy dress or robe that draped to the ground. She had on a yellow blouse and wore flip-flops. She certainly didn't have wings. We weren't in Los Angeles, the City of Angels. We were in downtown San Fransisco. The City is one of the most beautiful in the country, but arguably, one of the most Hedonistic.

But I don't know.

The good thing about not knowing is that I get to decide what I think. Maybe this lady does follow me around. Maybe she's the reason that Steve and I and the other farm kids never managed to kill ourselves or each other growing up. Maybe she followed me to rodeos and made sure I never got gored by a raging bull's horns. Maybe, just maybe, this lady had directed some surgeons' hands or doctors' minds over the years.

Or maybe she does follow me around and was finally tired of seeing me pine over a green rock.

But I don't know.

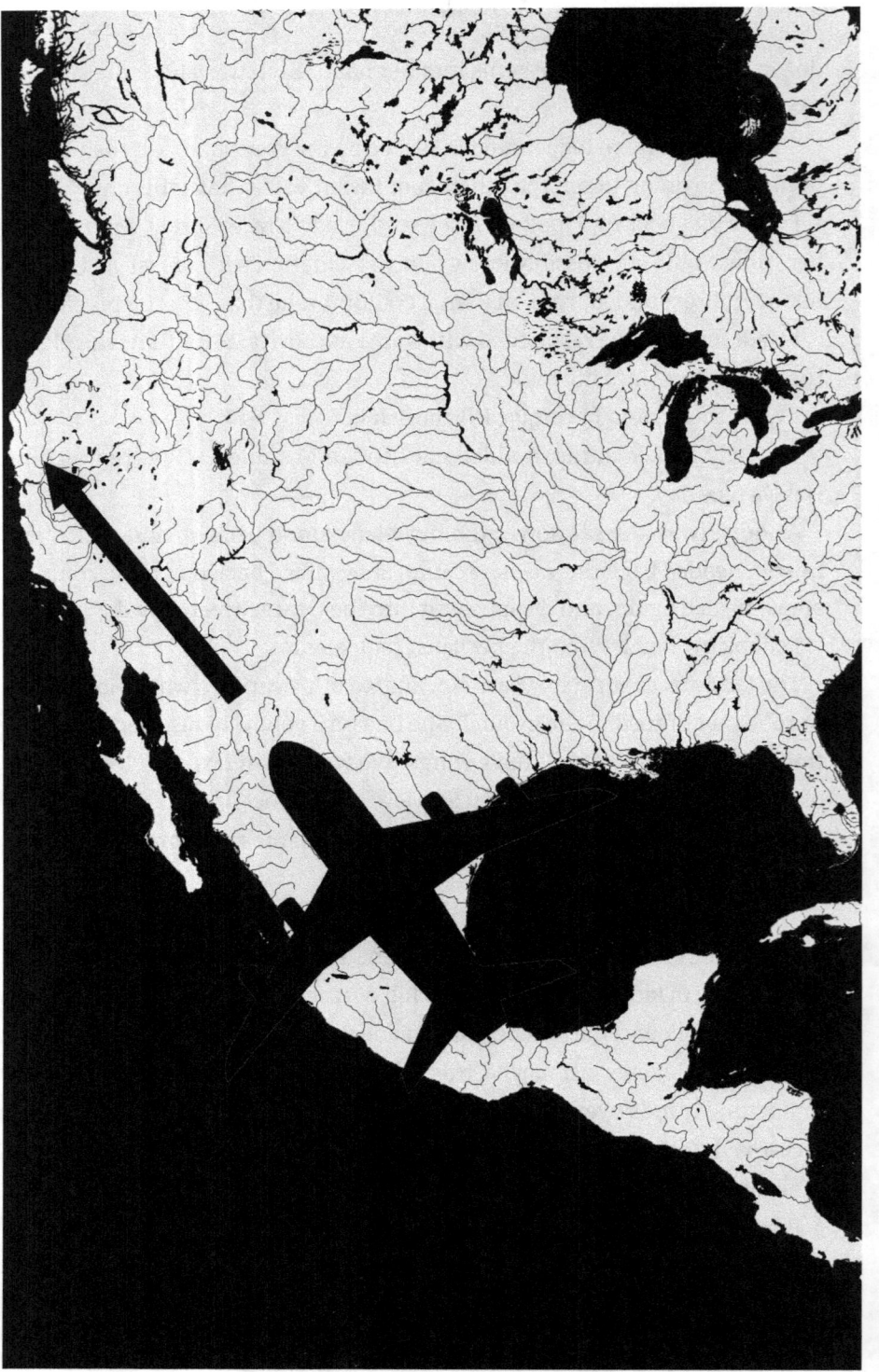

42

Home

I finished writing this book in the same place as I finished writing my last book—sitting in a lounge chair in a hut above the water in Bocas del Toro, Panama. We've been here for a month. We've been here many times and now have a number of local friends to visit and catch up with. I swim in the crystal clear water during the day. I fish, and I sit around and write. When we can, we take short boat rides to over-the-water restaurants for dinner.

Since I completed my last book, just over a year ago, here on this very island, Rhonda and I have covered some thousands of miles. We've spent over a month in Mexico and have eaten fish so fresh that it was swimming in the Sea of Cortez a few hours before it showed up on our plates. We cruised from Los Angeles, through the Mexican Riviera, and through the Panama Canal. We've bought coffee in Columbia and had oysters in Florida.

And here we are, sitting again in Panama, looking forward to dinner with Panamanian friends. I get to practice my Spanish, and they get to practice their English. The conversations will broaden our knowledge and understanding of the world. Travel, whether across town or across a continent, broadens us. It builds compassion. It opens minds. It fulfills something within us.

But we've been away for a month.

I've seen my country through the clouds of a jet's window and, on the horizon, across a ship's bow. I've seen it coming at me through a car's windshield and I've watched it disappear through a train's window. I've seen it under my feet on hikes and under my blanket on picnics.

It's always beautiful.

I've seen it many times, but it's never as lovely as when it comes into sight after you've been away for a long time, and it means home. ❤

About the Author

Hi! It's Rawge! I live with my wife, Rhonda, in a rural area outside Sacramento, CA, but I'm a native son of California's San Joaquin Valley. I was raised on a ranch and later worked in California's oil fields. In my mid-twenties, I moved to Northern California to attend the University of California, Davis. I just retired from a 34-year career as a professional wildlife biologist.

I took creative writing classes in community college and had always planned to write a book about the twists and turns in my life. The book (and many other things) was put into the file that we all have—you know, that thick file labeled "someday."

Early in the Pandemic, I ended up in a hospital for a month and on a ventilator. The prognosis was grim.

I guess being separated and quarantined from your loved ones and having a fat tube down your throat can change you! All the dreams I'd been saving for "someday" suddenly became urgent. I realized I came within a few heartbeats of running out of "somedays."

So, I'm no longer waiting for "someday."

I hug.

I say I love you.

I wrote another book!

Also by Rawge Jones

And There I Was... JUST MINDING MY OWN BUSINESS
It is a farm-to-fork-in-the-road memoir of a dirty-mouth ranch kid struggling to grow up and become a good person. The fifty-plus short stories contain laughs, tears, and occasional heartfelt smiles.

This easy-reading book is chock full of colorful characters, like a buxom Gypsy fortune teller, a sappy tree-hugger, a sneaky midnight Sancho lover, a feisty barnyard rooster, and many more.

Each entertaining chapter will leave you with something to think about long after the book is put away. Rawge's life of love, loss, bad decisions, and the inevitable passing of time is personal but universal to all of us.

www.rawge.com